A Prentice Hall Pocket Reader

WRITING ACROSS THE CURRICULUM

Edited by

Stephen Brown

University of Nevada, Las Vegas

PEARSON
Prentice Hall

Upper Saddle River, New Jersey 07458

© 2006 by PEARSON EDUCATION, INC.
Upper Saddle River, New Jersey 07458

10 9 8 7 6 5 4 3 2 1

ISBN 0-13-194210-7

Printed in the United States of America

CONTENTS

1

THE ENVIRONMENT

THE OBLIGATION TO ENDURE

Rachel Carson

The history of life on earth has been a history of interaction 1
between living things and their surroundings. To a large extent, the
physical form and the habits of the earth's vegetation and its animal
life have been molded by the environment. Considering the whole
span of earthly time, the opposite effect, in which life actually modifies its surroundings, has been relatively slight. Only within the
moment of time represented by the present century has one species—
man—acquired significant power to alter the nature of his world.

During the past quarter century this power has not only 2
increased to one of disturbing magnitude but it has changed in character. The most alarming of all man's assaults upon the environment
is the contamination of air, earth, rivers, and sea with dangerous and
even lethal materials. This pollution is for the most part irrecover-
able; the chain of evil it initiates not only in the world that must support life but in living tissues is for the most part irreversible. In this
now universal contamination of the environment, chemicals are the
sinister and little-recognized partners of radiation in changing the
very nature of the world—the very nature of its life. Strontium 90,
released through nuclear explosions into the air, comes to earth in
rain or drifts down as fallout, lodges in soil, enters into the grass or
corn or wheat grown there, and in time takes up its abode in the
bones of a human being, there to remain until his death. Similarly,
chemicals sprayed on croplands or forests or gardens lie long in soil,
entering into living organisms, passing from one to another in a
chain of poisoning and death. Or they pass mysteriously by underground streams until they emerge and, through the alchemy of air

and sunlight, combine into new forms that kill vegetation, sicken cattle, and work unknown harm on those who drink from once pure wells. As Albert Schweitzer has said, "Man can hardly even recognize the devils of his own creation."

It took hundreds of millions of years to produce the life that now 3
inhabits the earth—eons of time in which that developing and evolving and diversifying life reached a state of adjustment and balance with its surroundings. The environment, rigorously shaping and directing the life it supported, contained elements that were hostile as well as supporting. Certain rocks gave out dangerous radiation; even within the light of the sun, from which all life draws its energy, there were short-wave radiations with power to injure. Given time— time not in years but in millennia—life adjusts, and a balance has been reached. For time is the essential ingredient; but in the modern world there is no time.

The rapidity of change and the speed with which new situations 4
are created follow the impetuous and heedless pace of man rather than the deliberate pace of nature. Radiation is no longer merely the background radiation of rocks, the bombardment of cosmic rays, the ultraviolet of the sun that have existed before there was any life on earth; radiation is now the unnatural creation of man's tampering with the atom. The chemicals to which life is asked to make its adjustment are no longer merely the calcium and silica and copper and all the rest of the minerals washed out of the rocks and carried in rivers to the sea; they are the synthetic creations of man's inventive mind, brewed in his laboratories, and having no counterparts in nature.

To adjust to these chemicals would require time on the scale that 5
is nature's; it would require not merely the years of a man's life but the life of generations. And even this, were it by some miracle possible, would be futile, for the new chemicals come from our laboratories in an endless stream; almost five hundred annually find their way into actual use in the United States alone. The figure is staggering and its implications are not easily grasped—500 new chemicals to which the bodies of men and animals are required somehow to adapt each year, chemicals totally outside the limits of biologic experience.

Among them are many that are used in man's war against 6
nature. Since the mid-1940s over 200 basic chemicals have been created for use in killing insects, weeds, rodents, and other organisms described in the modern vernacular as "pests"; and they are sold under several thousand different brand names.

These sprays, dusts, and aerosols are now applied almost 7
universally to arms, gardens, forests, and homes—nonselective

chemicals that have the power to kill every insect, the "good" and the "bad," to still the song of birds and the leaping of fish in the streams, to coat the leaves with a deadly film, and to linger on in soil—all this though the intended target may be only a few weeds or insects. Can anyone believe it is possible to lay down such a barrage of poisons on the surface of the earth without making it unfit for all life? They should not be called "insecticides," but "biocides."

The whole process of spraying seems caught up in an endless 8 spiral. Since DDT was released for civilian use, a process of escalation has been going on in which ever more toxic materials must be found. This has happened because insects, in a triumphant vindication of Darwin's principle of the survival of the fittest, have evolved super races immune to the particular insecticide used, hence a deadlier one has always to be developed—and then a deadlier one than that. It has happened also because, for reasons to be described later, destructive insects often undergo a "flareback," or resurgence, after spraying, in numbers greater than before. Thus the chemical war is never won, and all life is caught in its violent crossfire.

Along with the possibility of the extinction of mankind by 9 nuclear war, the central problem of our age has therefore become the contamination of man's total environment with such substances of incredible potential for harm—substances that accumulate in the tissues of plants and animals and even penetrate the germ cells to shatter or alter the very material of heredity upon which the shape of the future depends.

Some would-be architects of our future look toward a time when 10 it will be possible to alter the human germ plasm by design. But we may easily be doing so now by inadvertence, for many chemicals, like radiation, bring about gene mutations. It is ironic to think that man might determine his own future by something so seemingly trivial as the choice of an insect spray.

All this has been risked—for what? Future historians may well be 11 amazed by our distorted sense of proportion. How could intelligent beings seek to control a few unwanted species by a method that contaminated the entire environment and brought the threat of disease and death even to their own kind? Yet this is precisely what we have done. We have done it, moreover, for reasons that collapse the moment we examine them. We are told that the enormous and expanding use of pesticides is necessary to maintain farm production. Yet is our real problem not one of *overproduction?* Our farms, despite measures to remove acreages from production and to pay farmers *not* to produce, have yielded such a staggering excess of crops that the

American taxpayer in 1962 is paying out more than one billion dollars a year as the total carrying cost of the surplus-food storage program. And is the situation helped when one branch of the Agriculture Department tries to reduce production while another states, as it did in 1958, "It is believed generally that reduction of crop acreages under provisions of the Soil Bank will stimulate interest in use of chemicals to obtain maximum production on the land retained in crops"?

All this is not to say there is no insect problem and no need of 12 control. I am saying, rather, that control must be geared to realities, not to mythical situations, and that the methods employed must be such that they do not destroy us along with the insects.

The problem whose attempted solution has brought such a train 13 of disaster in its wake is an accompaniment of our modern way of life. Long before the age of man, insects inhabited the earth—a group of extraordinarily varied and adaptable beings. Over the course of time since man's advent, a small percentage of the more than half a million species of insects have come into conflict with human welfare in two principal ways: as competitors for the food supply and as carriers of human disease.

Disease-carrying insects become important where human beings 14 are crowded together, especially under conditions where sanitation is poor, as in time of natural disaster or war or in situations of extreme poverty and deprivation. Then control of some sort becomes necessary. It is a sobering fact, however, as we shall presently see, that the method of massive chemical control has had only limited success, and also threatens to worsen the very conditions it is intended to curb.

Under primitive agricultural conditions the farmer had few 15 insect problems. These arose with the intensification of agriculture—the devotion of immense acreages to a single crop. Such a system set the stage for explosive increases in specific insect populations. Single-crop farming does not take advantage of the principles by which nature works; it is agriculture as an engineer might conceive it to be. Nature has introduced great variety into the landscape, but man has displayed a passion for simplifying it. Thus he undoes the built-in checks and balances by which nature holds the species within bounds. One important natural check is a limit on the amount of suitable habitat for each species. Obviously then, an insect that lives on wheat can build up its population to much higher levels on a farm devoted to wheat than on one in which wheat is intermingled with other crops to which the insect is not adapted.

The same thing happens in other situations. A generation or 16
more ago, the towns of large areas of the United States lined their
streets with the noble elm tree. Now the beauty they hopefully created is threatened with complete destruction as disease sweeps
through the elms, carried by a beetle that would have only limited
chance to build up large populations and to spread from tree to tree
if the elms were only occasional trees in a richly diversified planting.

Another factor in the modern insect problem is one that must be 17
viewed against a background of geologic and human history: the
spreading of thousands of different kinds of organisms from their
native homes to invade new territories. This worldwide migration
has been studied and graphically described by the British ecologist
Charles Elton in his recent book *The Ecology of Invasions*. During the
Cretaceous Period, some hundred million years ago, flooding seas
cut many land bridges between continents and living things found
themselves confined in what Elton calls "colossal separate nature
reserves." There, isolated from others of their kind, they developed
many new species. When some of the land masses were joined again,
about 15 million years ago, these species began to move out into new
territories—a movement that is not only still in progress but is now
receiving considerable assistance from man.

The importation of plants is the primary agent in the modern 18
spread of species, for animals have almost invariably gone along with
the plants, quarantine being a comparatively recent and not completely effective innovation. The United States Office of Plant
Introduction alone has introduced almost 200,000 species and varieties
of plants from all over the world. Nearly half of the 180 or so major
insect enemies of plants in the United States are accidental imports
from abroad, and most of them have come as hitchhikers on plants.

In new territory, out of reach of the restraining hand of the nat- 19
ural enemies that kept down its numbers in its native land, an invading plant or animal is able to become enormously abundant. Thus it
is no accident that our most troublesome insects are introduced
species.

These invasions, both the naturally occurring and those depen- 20
dent on human assistance, are likely to continue indefinitely.
Quarantine and massive chemical campaigns are only extremely
expensive ways of buying time. We are faced, according to Dr. Elton,
"with a life-and-death need not just to find new technological means
of suppressing this plant or that animal"; instead we need the basic
knowledge of animal populations and their relations to their sur-

roundings that will "promote an even balance and damp down the explosive power of outbreaks and new invasions."

Much of the necessary knowledge is now available but we do not use it. We train ecologists in our universities and even employ them in our governmental agencies but we seldom take their advice. We allow the chemical death rain to fall as though there were no alternatives, whereas in fact there are many, and our ingenuity could soon discover many more if given opportunity.

Have we fallen into a mesmerized state that makes us accept as inevitable that which is inferior or detrimental, as though having lost the will or the vision to demand that which is good? Such thinking, in the words of the ecologist Paul Shepard, "idealizes life with only its head out of water, inches above the limits of toleration of the corruption of its own environment. . . . Why should we tolerate a diet of weak poisons, a home in insipid surroundings, a circle of acquaintances who are not quite our enemies, the noise of motors with just enough relief to prevent insanity? Who would want to live in a world which is just not quite fatal?"

Yet such a world is pressed upon us. The crusade to create a chemically sterile, insect-free world seems to have engendered a fanatic zeal on the part of many specialists and most of the so-called control agencies. On every hand there is evidence that those engaged in spraying operations exercise a ruthless power. "The regulatory entomologists . . . function as prosecutor, judge and jury, tax assessor and collector and sheriff to enforce their own orders," said Connecticut entomologist Neely Turner. The most flagrant abuses go unchecked in both state and federal agencies.

It is not my contention that chemical insecticides must never be used. I do contend that we have put poisonous and biologically potent chemicals indiscriminately into the hands of persons largely or wholly ignorant of their potentials for harm. We have subjected enormous numbers of people to contact with these poisons, without their consent and often without their knowledge. If the Bill of Rights contains no guarantee that a citizen shall be secure against lethal poisons distributed either by private individuals or by public officials, it is surely only because our forefathers, despite their considerable wisdom and foresight, could conceive of no such problem.

I contend, furthermore, that we have allowed these chemicals to be used with little or no advance investigation of their effect on soil, water, wildlife, and man himself. Future generations are unlikely to condone our lack of prudent concern for the integrity of the natural world that supports all life.

There is still very limited awareness of the nature of the threat. 26 This is an era of specialists, each of whom sees his own problem and is unaware of or intolerant of the larger frame into which it fits. It is also an era dominated by industry, in which the right to make a dollar at whatever cost is seldom challenged. When the public protests, confronted with some obvious evidence of damaging results of pesticide applications, it is fed little tranquilizing pills of half truth. We urgently need an end to these false assurances, to the sugar coating of unpalatable facts. It is the public that is being asked to assume the risks that the insect controllers calculate. The public must decide whether it wishes to continue on the present road, and it can do so only when in full possession of the facts. In the words of Jean Rostand, "The obligation to endure gives us the right to know."

THE NEXT STEP
FOR U.S. CLIMATE CHANGE POLICY

Warwick McKibbin
Peter Wilcoxen

During the recent European summit, President Bush faced criti- 1
cism from his European counterparts, from protestors and from
much of the world media for his stance on rejecting the Kyoto
Protocol. Why is there almost universal criticism despite the fact that
the Bush administration has done the world a favor by abandoning
the Kyoto Protocol? The approach of fixed targets and timetables for
emissions reduction at an unknown economic cost is an infeasible
and undesirable approach to climate change. The Protocol never had
any chance of ratification. The reason for the outcry is that rather
than put in place a better alternative to Kyoto, the Bush administration has so far left a vacuum in place of a climate change response. If
the administration moves quickly to put a more realistic policy on the
table, then the focus of the global reaction can be shifted from outrage
to reasoned debate. Abandoning the Kyoto Protocol could be the
most important and positive environmental legacy of the Bush
administration. The European summit was the first opportunity to
act, but it was lost. The next opportunity is at the COP6(II) negotiations to be held in Bonn in July.

Being realistic means discarding a couple of notions cherished by 2
the ideologically pure at either end of the political spectrum. The first
thing to go should be the claim that climate change is not a problem.
It is quite clear that human activity is raising global concentrations of
carbon dioxide. While climatologists disagree about how much
warming will occur and when it will happen, virtually no one seriously suggests that we can emit as much carbon dioxide as we want
into the atmosphere without any adverse consequences.

The second notion to go should be the one at the other end of the 3
spectrum: The idea that climate change is such an overwhelming
problem that it must be stopped no matter what the cost. Frankly, too
little is known about the damages caused by climate change and the
costs of reducing emissions to draw this conclusion. To pretend that
climate policy doesn't need to take costs into consideration is to guarantee that any climate change treaty will be rejected by the US Senate
as well as by many other governments.

A good way to think about the climate change problem is by analogy to driving in the rain. Both involve risk: Rain increases the chance of being involved in a serious accident and carbon dioxide emissions increase the chance of a serious climate problem. The right response to risks like these is prudence: When it is raining, people drive more carefully and avoid unnecessary trips. Likewise, in the face of a potential climate problem, a sensible thing to do would be to slow the growth of carbon dioxide emissions. In neither case is it practical to escape the risk entirely. Few people would be in favor of a law prohibiting driving in the rain under any circumstances. Similarly, few people would be willing to accept sharp reductions in fossil fuel use today simply because it might cause a problem sometime in the future.

After tossing the ideological baggage overboard, what might prudent and realistic governments do about climate change? The answer is to look for a global warming policy with three key features. First, the policy should slow down carbon dioxide emissions where it is cost-effective to do so. Second, the policy should involve some mechanism for compensating those who will be hurt economically. Third, since climate change is a global problem, any solution will require a high degree of consensus both domestically and internationally. However, consensus is the operative word; it is not realistic to think that a rigid global regulatory regime for greenhouse policy can ever be implemented. Few countries want to relinquish sovereignty over setting their own policies, especially when the policies in question can have large economic effects.

We have set out such a policy in a recent Brookings Policy Brief. Our proposed permit trading system is much like the one now used to control sulphur emissions. The main difference would be that the market would include a mechanism that would prevent the price of a permit from exceeding a specified threshold. The threshold price would be set for ten years at a time. Thus emissions would be allowed to vary over time and not be fixed as under the Kyoto Protocol. There are mechanisms in the detailed proposal that allow medium term targets and a market to price these. The permits would be given freely to each citizen and to existing emitters to grandfather emissions. These would be tradable in an open market. Any additional permits that would be required to keep the price from exceeding the threshold would be sold by the government in that year. By raising the price of carbon, the net effect of the policy would be to discourage increases in emissions, and to encourage reductions where they are cost-effective, but without levying a sudden multi-billion dollar burden on fuel users. This would be a significant, realistic step toward controlling climate change.

A key feature of the policy is that it is flexible. The permit price could be adjusted as needed when better information becomes available on the seriousness of climate change and the cost of reducing emissions. 7

As a unilateral policy this is feasible. Success would encourage other countries to join a more coordinated system. A country could join a multilateral system by adopting the policy domestically and no international negotiations would be required. If the same permit price were chosen in all countries, the system would reach a very efficient and low-cost outcome—very similar to that from a global permit trading system but without the problems associated with international permit trading. Flexibility is crucial because it is clear from current negotiations that only a small subset of countries would agree to be initial participants in a climate change treaty. 8

It is time for the Bush administration to offer realistic alternatives to the Kyoto Protocol. The debate must move away from ideological battles over impractical goals and un-implementable policies to a discussion of policies that could be concrete but cost-effective steps to slow the growth of carbon dioxide emissions. 9

U.S. FOREST CONSERVATION MAY INCREASE DEFORESTATION ELSEWHERE

Pam Mayfield

A new study examining the future of world timber markets sug- 1
gests that forest conservation efforts in North America and Europe
could lead to increased deforestation in threatened tropical forests.
The study predicts the loss of one hectare (2.47 acres) of previously
inaccessible forest in Asia, South America, Africa, and the former
Soviet Union for every twenty hectares set aside and protected in
North America and Europe. In short, the forests saved in Europe and
America are replaced by the felling of trees elsewhere.

"A small amount of forest conservation here can have negative 2
worldwide effects," said Brent Sohngen, co-author of the study and
assistant professor of agricultural, environmental, and development
economics at Ohio State University.

For the most part, foresters ignore timber supplies available in 3
many of the world's tropical forests because these areas are expensive to harvest at current prices. However, Sohngen's models predict
this situation could change if forest conservation in North America
and Europe raises world prices. "North America currently produces
35 percent of global timber. Conserving only 5 to 10 percent of tim-
berland in a region that supplies such a large proportion of global
harvests will increase harvests elsewhere, including tropical forests
that presently are inaccessible."

Many scientists are concerned about the possible ecological 4
implications of the decline of tropical forests: The loss of biodiversity
and undiscovered species, increased soil erosion, and the reduction
of plants that remove CO_2 from the atmosphere. The United Nations
Food and Agriculture Organization points out that as of 1990, the
tropics contained 60 percent of the world's inaccessible forests—over
800 million hectares, nearly twice the area of the state of Texas.

Sohngen conducted the study with Robert Mendelsohn, a pro- 5
fessor of forestry at Yale University, and Roger Sedjo, a senior fellow
at Resources for the Future in Washington, DC. The results were published in a recent issue of the *American Journal of Agricultural
Economics*. The researchers developed a variety of models that examined how worldwide demand for timber might affect the conservation of forests across the globe between 1995 and 2135. They
examined both current and predicted global timber supply, demand,

prices, and harvest costs. Their analyses accounted for supply and harvest differences across several geographic regions and compared regeneration and forest development costs.

Part of the researchers' model examined two possible scenarios. 6 The first assumes that 5 percent of North American and European forests will be preserved and the second suggests 10 percent of these forests will be saved.

Both scenarios predict that these set-asides would increase 7 worldwide timber prices by 1 to 2 percent, while increasing timber harvests in other parts of the world by 1 percent. In the 5 percent scenario, the model predicts 1.4 million hectares of previously economically inaccessible forests are harvested elsewhere, and in the 10 percent case, an additional 2 million hectares of inaccessible forests are harvested elsewhere. These additional timber harvests would likely occur in tropical areas, Sohngen said.

Sohngen said simple economics helps explain why forest conser- 8 vation in North America and Europe may increase deforestation in the tropics and elsewhere. "As supply decreases through increased conservation efforts in North America, timber prices will rise, making it economically feasible to harvest trees from areas where it was previously too expensive," he said.

However, Sohngen said that the same economics that create this 9 predicament could also play a role in solving it. Increased tropical harvests require expansion into areas of forest that have never been cut before. This demands the construction of roads and the transportation of equipment and labor into remote places. These outlays would be quite costly. However, harvesting in already developed forests throughout the world eliminates these construction costs, resulting in higher profits. This increased profit margin acts as an incentive for better management of these areas.

Sohngen pointed out, however, that government tax breaks and 10 subsidies for timber companies often work against sound management of forest lands. Many federal governments, including that of the United States, pay for new road construction to make forests accessible. Relieving timber companies of the construction expenses enables them to harvest affordably in previously inaccessible areas.

The model shows that these access costs play a critical role in the 11 amount of inaccessible tropical forests that are lost to timber harvesting. Low access costs predict a loss of 150 million hectares over the next fifty to seventy-five years, while high access costs lower that figure to 50 million hectares. Although none of their scenarios predicts the elimination of timber harvests in the world's tropical forests,

Sohngen said he believes most of the increase in timber production will come from second- and third-growth forests and from tree plantations planted specifically for timber. In the tropics, these plantations have primarily been developed on degraded agricultural land.

Sohngen noted that their predictions only apply to forest loss [12] due to timber harvesting, which the model suggests plays only a minor role in tropical deforestation. "Other local factors not considered by this model—such as increasing development of agriculture—may still pose a threat."

BIG MAC AND THE TROPICAL FORESTS

Joseph K. Skinner

Hello, fast-food chains.   1

Goodbye, tropical forests.   2

Sound like an odd connection? The "free-market" economy has   3
led to results even stranger than this, but perhaps none have been as
environmentally devastating.

These are the harsh facts: the tropical forests are being leveled for   4
commercial purposes at the rate of 150,000 square kilometers a year,
an area the size of England and Wales combined.[1]

At this rate, the world's tropical forests could be entirely   5
destroyed within seventy-three years. Already as much as a fifth or a
quarter of the huge Amazon forest, which constitutes a third of the
world's total rain forest, has been cut, and the rate of destruction is
accelerating. And nearly two thirds of the Central American forests
have been cleared or severely degraded since 1950.

Tropical forests, which cover only 7 percent of the Earth's land   6
surface (it used to be 12 percent), support half the species of the
world's living things. Due to their destruction, "We are surely losing
one or more species a day right now out of the five million (mini-
mum figure) on Earth," says Norman Myers, author of numerous
books and articles on the subject and consultant to the World Bank
and the World Wildlife Fund. "By the time ecological equilibrium is
restored, at least one-quarter of all species will have disappeared,
probably a third, and conceivably even more. . . . If this pattern continues, it could mean the demise of two million species by the middle of next century." Myers calls the destruction of the tropical forests
"one of the greatest biological debacles to occur on the face of the
Earth." Looking at the effects it will have on the course of biological
evolution, Myers says:

> The impending upheaval in evolution's course could rank as
> one of the greatest biological revolutions of paleontological time.
> It will equal in scale and significance the development of aerobic
> respiration, the emergence of flowering plants, and the arrival of
> limbed animals. But of course the prospective degradation of

---

[1] Jean-Paul Londley, "Tropical Forests resources." FAO Forestry Paper 30 (Rome: FAO, 1982).

many evolutionary capacities will be an impoverishing, not a creative, phenomenon.[2]

In other words, such rapid destruction will vacate so many 7 niches so suddenly that a "pest and weed" ecology, consisting of a relatively few opportunistic species (rats, roaches, and the like) will be created.

Beyond this—as if it weren't enough—such destruction could 8 well have cataclysmic effects on the Earth's weather patterns, causing, for example, an irreversible desertification of the North American grain belt. Although the scope of the so-called greenhouse effect—in which rising levels of carbon dioxide in the atmosphere heat the planet by preventing infrared radiation from escaping into space—is still being debated within the scientific community, it is not at all extreme to suppose that the fires set to clear tropical forests will contribute greatly to this increase in atmospheric CO_2 and thereby to untold and possibly devastating changes in the world's weather systems.

Big Mac Attack

So what does beef, that staple of the fast-food chains and of the 9 North American diet in general, have to do with it?

It used to be, back in 1960, that the United States imported prac- 10 tically no beef. That was a time when North Americans were consuming a "mere" 85 pounds of beef per person per year. By 1980 this was up to 134 pounds per person per year. Concomitant with this increase in consumption, the United States began to import beef, so that by 1981 some 800,000 tons were coming in from abroad, 17 percent of it from tropical Latin America and three fourths of that from Central America. Since fast-food chains have been steadily expanding and now are a $5-billion-a-year business, accounting for 25 percent of all the beef consumed in the United States, the connections between the fast-food empire and tropical beef are clear.

---

[2] There are amazingly few scientists in the world with broad enough expertise to accurately assess the widest implications of tropical deforestation; Norman Myers is one of them. His books include *The Sinking Ark* (Oxford: Pergamon Press, 1979). See also *Conversion of Moist Tropical Forests* (Washington, D.C.: National Academy of Sciences, 1980), "The End of the Line," *Natural History* 94, no. 2 (February 1985), and "The Hamburger Connection," *Ambio* 10, no. 1 (1981). I have used Myers extensively in the preparation of this article. The quotes in this paragraph are from "The Hamburger Connection," pp. 3, 4, 5.

Cattle ranching is "by far the major factor in forest destruction in [11] tropical Latin America," says Myers. "Large fast-food outlets in the U.S. and Europe foster the clearance of forests to produce cheap beef."[3]

And cheap it is, compared to North American beef: by 1978 the [12] average price of beef imported from Central America was $1.47/kg, while similar North American beef cost $3.30/kg.

Cheap, that is, for North Americans, but not for Central [13] Americans. Central Americans cannot afford their own beef. Whereas beef production in Costa Rica increased twofold between 1959 and 1972, per capita consumption of beef in that country went down from 30 lbs. a year to 19. In Honduras, beef production increased by 300 percent between 1965 and 1975, but consumption decreased from 12 lbs. per capita per year to 10. So, although two thirds of Central America's arable land is in cattle, local consumption of beef is decreasing; the average domestic cat in the United States now consumes more beef than the average Central American.[4]

Brazilian government figures show that 38 percent of all defor- [14] estation in the Brazilian Amazon between 1966 and 1975 was attrib- utable to large-scale cattle ranching. Although the presence of hoof-and-mouth disease among Brazilian cattle has forced U.S. law- makers to prohibit the importation of chilled or frozen Brazilian beef, the United States imports $46 million per year of cooked Brazilian beef, which goes into canned products; over 80 percent of Brazilian beef is still exported, most of it to Western Europe, where no such prohibition exists.

At present rates, all remaining Central American forests will [15] have been eliminated by 1990. The cattle ranching largely responsi- ble for this is in itself highly inefficient: as erosion and nutrient leach- ing eat away the soil, production drops from an average one head per hectare—measly in any case—to a pitiful one head per five to seven hectares within five to ten years. A typical tropical cattle ranch employs only one person per 2,000 head, and meat production barely reaches 50 lbs./acre/year. In Northern Europe, in farms that do not use imported feed, it is over 500 lbs./acre/year.

This real-term inefficiency does not translate into bad business, [16] however, for although there are some absentee landowners who

---

[3] Myers, "End of the Line," p. 2.

[4] See James Nations and Daniel I. Komer, "Rainforests and the Hamburger Society," *Environment* 25, no. 3 (April 1983).

engage in ranching for the prestige of it and are not particularly interested in turning large profits, others find bank loans for growing beef for export readily forthcoming, and get much help and encouragement from such organizations as the Pan American Health Organization, the Organization of American States, the U.S. Department of Agriculture, and U.S. AID, without whose technical assistance "cattle production in the American tropics would be unprofitable, if not impossible."[5] The ultimate big winner appears to be the United States, where increased imports of Central American beef are said to have done more to stem inflation than any other single government initiative.

"On the good land, which could support a large population, you have the rich cattle owners, and on the steep slopes, which should be left in forest, you have the poor farmers," says Gerardo Budowski, director of the Tropical Agricultural Research and Training Center in Turrialba, Costa Rica. "It is still good business to clear virgin forest in order to fatten cattle for, say, five to eight years and then abandon it."[6]

(Ironically, on a trip I made in 1981 to Morazán, a Salvadoran province largely under control of FMLN guerrillas, I inquired into the guerilla diet and discovered that beef, expropriated from the cattle ranches, was a popular staple.)

Swift-Armour's Swift Armor

The rain forest ecosystem, the oldest on Earth, is extremely complex and delicate. In spite of all the greenery one sees there, it is a myth that rain forest soil is rich. It is actually quite poor, leached of all nutrients save the most insoluble (such as iron oxides, which give lateritic soil—the most common soil type found there—its red color). Rather, the ecosystem of the rain forest is a "closed" one, in which the nutrients are to be found in the biomass, that is, in the living canopy of plants and in the thin layer of humus on the ground that is formed from the matter shed by the canopy. Hence the shallow-rootedness of most tropical forest plant species. Since the soil itself cannot replenish nutrients, nutrient recycling is what keeps the system going.

Now, what happens when the big cattle ranchers, under the auspices of the Swift-Armour Meat Packing Co., or United Brands, or the

---

[5] Nations and Komer, "Rainforests and the Hamburger Society," p. 17.

[6] Catherine Caufield, "The Rain Forests," *New Yorker* (January 14, 1985), p. 42. This excellent article was later incorporated in a book, *In the Rainforest* (New York: Knopf, 1985).

King Ranch, sling a huge chain between two enormous tractors, level a few tens of thousands of acres of tropical forest, burn the debris, fly a plane over to seed the ash with guinea grass, and then run their cattle on the newly created grasslands?[7]

For the first three years or so the grass grows like crazy, up to an 21 inch a day, thriving on all that former biomass. After that, things go quickly downhill: the ash becomes eroded and leached, the soil becomes exposed and hardens to the consistency of brick, and the area becomes useless to agriculture. Nor does it ever regain anything near its former state. The Amazon is rising perceptibly as a result of the increased runoff due to deforestation.

Tractor-and-chain is only one way of clearing the land. Another 22 common technique involves the use of herbicides such as Tordon, 2, 4-D, and 2,4,5-T (Agent Orange). The dioxin found in Agent Orange can be extremely toxic to animal life and is very persistent in the environment.

Tordon, since it leaves a residue deadly to all broad-leaved 23 plants, renders the deforested area poisonous to all plants except grasses; consequently, even if they wanted to, ranchers could not plant soil-enriching legumes in the treated areas, a step which many agronomists recommend for keeping the land productive for at least a little longer.

The scale of such operations is a far cry from the traditional 24 slash-and-burn practiced by native jungle groups, which is done on a scale small enough so that the forest can successfully reclaim the farmed areas. Such groups, incidentally, are also being decimated by cattle interests in Brazil and Paraguay—as missionaries, human rights groups, and cattlemen themselves will attest.

Capital's "manifest destiny" has traditionally shown little con- 25 cern for the lives of trees or birds or Indians, or anything else which interferes with immediate profitability, but the current carving of holes in the gene pool by big agribusiness seems particularly short-sighted. Since the tropical forests contain two thirds of the world's genetic resources, their destruction will leave an enormous void in the pool of genes necessary for the creation of new agricultural hybrids. This is not to mention the many plants as yet undiscovered—there could be up to 15,000 unknown species in South America

---

[7] Other multinationals with interests in meat packing and cattle ranching in tropical Latin America include Armour-Dial International, Goodyear Tire and Rubber Co., and Gulf and Western Industries, Inc. See Roger Burbach and Patricia Flynn, *Agribusiness in the Americas* (New York: Monthly Review Press, 1980).

alone—which may in themselves contain remarkable properties. (In writing about alkaloids found in the Madagascar periwinkle which have recently revolutionized the treatment of leukemia and Hodgkin's disease, British biochemist John Humphreys said: "If this plant had not been analyzed, not even a chemist's wildest ravings would have hinted that such structures would be pharmacologically active."[8] Ninety percent of Madagascar's forests have been cut.)

But there is no small truth in Indonesian Minister for Environment and Development Emil Salim's complaint that the "South is asked to conserve genes while the other fellow, in the North, is consuming things that force us to destroy the genes in the South."[9]

Where's the Beef?

The marketing of beef imported into the United States is extremely complex, and the beef itself ends up in everything from hot dogs to canned soup. Fresh meat is exported in refrigerated container ships to points of entry, where it is inspected by the U.S. Department of Agriculture. Once inspected, it is no longer required to be labeled "imported."[10] From there it goes into the hands of customhouse brokers and meat packers, often changing hands many times; and from there it goes to the fast-food chains or the food processors. The financial structures behind this empire are even more complex, involving governments and quasipublic agencies, such as the Export-Import Bank and the Overseas Private Investment Corporation, as well as the World Bank and the Inter-American Development Bank, all of which encourage cattle raising in the forest lands. (Brazilian government incentives to cattle ranching in Amazonia include a 50 percent income-tax rebate on ranchers' investments elsewhere in Brazil, tax holidays of up to ten years, loans with negative interest rates in real terms, and exemptions from sales taxes and import duties. Although these incentives were deemed excessive and since 1979 no longer apply to new ranches, they still continue for existing ones. This cost the Brazilian government $63,000 for each ranching job created.)

---

[8] Quoted in Caulfield, "Rain Forests," p. 60.

[9] Caulfield, "Rain Forests," p. 100.

[10] This is one way McDonald's, for example, can claim not to use foreign beef. For a full treatment of McDonald's, see M. Boas and S. Chain, *Big Mac: The Unauthorized Story of McDonald's* (New York: New American Library, 1976).

Beef production in the tropics may be profitable for the few, but 28 it is taking place at enormous cost for the majority and for the planet as a whole. Apart from the environmental destruction, it is a poor converter of energy to protein and provides few benefits for the vast majority of tropical peoples in terms of employment or food. What they require are labor-intensive, multiple-cropping systems.

The world is obviously hostage to an ethic which puts short-term 29 profitability above all else, and such catastrophes as the wholesale destruction of the tropical forests and the continued impoverishment of their peoples are bound to occur as long as this ethic rules.

THE UGLY GUZZLERS

Derrick Z. Jackson

Europe's latest stereotype of the ugly American is the lazy fat 1
guy mowing down the trees in his personal Sherman tank. It is the
paranoid ninety-pound woman whose forehead barely crests over
the steering wheel of her three-ton cocoon. We are the nation of insuf-
ferable whiners about our subsidized price of petrol.

"You Americans and your giant cars," a British hiker said to us at 2
a Swiss alpine hut. "Why do you need those things?"

"Your cars are monstrous," said a German telecommunications 3
businessman on a train out of Frankfurt. "It's unbelievable that anyone would need a car the size you drive."

"Doesn't anyone care about the environment back in the States?" 4
asked one of our hosts in rural northern Germany.

President Bush was held in particular scorn by nearly every 5
European we met on a recent vacation to Switzerland and Germany.
His pulling out of the Kyoto accords on global warming was viewed
as an arrogant declaration of who owns the White House. As the
British hiker put it, "You are the United States of Oil."

The sneer we show to the world on the environment is sure to 6
worsen before it gets better. Last month a US Department of
Transportation report found that sport utility vehicles (SUVs), minivans, and pickup trucks now account for 51 percent of new vehicle
sales. The report also found that those vehicles, classified as light-
duty trucks, now account for more miles driven on American roads
than do passenger cars.

The effects of these gas guzzlers are becoming as choking as a 7
sheet of smog. Preliminary federal figures released last month found
that in the last three years, carbon dixoide emissions from transportation have for the first time surpassed the CO_2 emissions from
industrial sources. Carbon dioxide emissions are a leading contribu-
tor to global warming.

In greater Washington, DC, the percentage of SUVs has grown 8
from 15 percent of personal vehicles to 25 percent in the last five
years. The spewing of emissions from these cars that get less than
twenty miles a gallon will likely force the region over its acceptable
limits for air pollution. If the region goes over the limit, it cannot ini-
tiate new road and bridge projects.

Just as the size of the American house has grown even as the size 9 of the American family has shrunk, the size of our cars has mushroomed without an excusable rationale. Detroit keeps telling us we need sport utility vehicles to roar over mountains and plow through lakes. The dream of leaving one's tire tracks on rugged landscapes has allowed automakers to charge on average 58 percent more for SUVs than for passenger cars.

But in the report from the Department of Transportation, authors 10 Kara Maria Kockelman and Yong Zhao of the University of Texas found that sport utility vehicles are used no more than passenger cars for recreational purposes.

Years ago, the auto lobby succeeded in avoiding miles-per-gallon 11 standards on SUVs, minivans, and pickup trucks by having them classified as cargo vehicles. But the authors of the Department of Transportation report found "no strong indication that minivans and SUV's are used as 'work' vehicles." They even found that "pickups are more popular among households than they were twenty years ago when American life was less urban, so it is not clear that pickups are performing unusual services either."

It is clear what unusual damage the giant American car is doing. 12 The Europeans we met were quick to say they were not perfect, with a highly publicized debate this spring in northern Germany over nuclear waste. What they could not understand was the extent of America's ignorance, denial, or selfishness about a problem we could easily work on by raising fuel standards.

We are only 6 percent of the world's population, but we produce 13 about a quarter of the world's greenhouse gases. This week, it was reported that a panel appointed by the National Academy of Sciences says that fuel efficiency can be increased. But, fitting of a panel backed by Bush, the report set no specific goals. The panel included no environmentalists, only engineers and consultants tied to the oil and auto industries.

That does not inspire much hope of a serious raising of stan- 14 dards. It will surely inspire more shaking of heads from our European friends. In their minds American men are going to grow fatter and women even more tiny as our cars grow from tanks into aircraft carriers. Americans seem incapable of looking themselves in the mirror and declaring how ugly they are.

2

THE MEDIA

PROPAGANDA UNDER A DICTATORSHIP

Aldous Huxley

At his trial after the Second World War, Hitler's Minister for [1] Armaments, Albert Speer, delivered a long speech in which, with remarkable acuteness, he described the Nazi tyranny and analyzed its methods. "Hitler's dictatorship," he said, "differed in one fundamental point from all its predecessors in history. It was the first dictatorship in the present period of modern technical development, a dictatorship which made complete use of all technical means for the domination of its own country. Through technical devices like the radio and the loudspeaker, eighty million people were deprived of independent thought. It was thereby possible to subject them to the will of one man.... Earlier dictators needed highly qualified assistants even at the lowest level—men who could think and act independently. The totalitarian system in the period of modern technical development can dispense with such men; thanks to modern methods of communication, it is possible to mechanize the lower leadership. As a result of this there has arisen the new type of the uncritical recipient of orders."

In the Brave New World of my prophetic fable technology had [2] advanced far beyond the point it had reached in Hitler's day; consequently the recipients of orders were far less critical than their Nazi counterparts, far more obedient to the order-giving elite. Moreover, they had been genetically standardized and postnatally conditioned to perform their subordinate functions, and could therefore be depended upon to behave almost as predictably as machines.... This conditioning of "the lower leadership" is already going on under the Communist dictatorships. The Chinese and the Russians

23

are not relying merely on the indirect effects of advancing technology; they are working directly on the psychophysical organisms of their lower leaders, subjecting minds and bodies to a system of ruthless and, from all accounts, highly effective conditioning. "Many a man," said Speer, "has been haunted by the nightmare that one day nations might be dominated by technical means. That nightmare was almost realized in Hitler's totalitarian system." Almost, but not quite. The Nazis did not have time—and perhaps did not have the intelligence and the necessary knowledge—to brainwash and condition their lower leadership. This, it may be, is one of the reasons why they failed.

Since Hitler's day the armory of technical devices at the disposal 3 of the would-be dictator has been considerably enlarged. As well as the radio, the loudspeaker, the moving picture camera and the rotary press, the contemporary propagandist can make use of television to broadcast the image as well as the voice of his client, and can record both image and voice on spools of magnetic tape. Thanks to technological progress, Big Brother can now be almost as omnipresent as God. Nor is it only on the technical front that the hand of the would-be dictator has been strengthened. Since Hitler's day a great deal of work has been carried out in those fields of applied psychology and neurology which are the special province of the propagandist, the indoctrinator and the brainwasher. In the past these specialists in the art of changing people's minds were empiricists. By a method of trial and error they had worked out a number of techniques and procedures, which they used very effectively without, however, knowing precisely why they were effective. Today the art of mind-control is in process of becoming a science. The practitioners of this science know what they are doing and why. They are guided in their work by theories and hypotheses solidly established on a massive foundation of experimental evidence. Thanks to the new insights and the new techniques made possible by these insights, the nightmare that was "all but realized in Hitler's totalitarian system" may soon be completely realizable.

But before we discuss these new insights and techniques let us 4 take a look at the nightmare that so nearly came true in Nazi Germany. What were the methods used by Hitler and Goebbels[1] for "depriving eighty million people of independent thought and subjecting them to the will of one man"? And what was the theory of

---

[1] *Joseph Paul Goebbels* (1897–1945): the propaganda minister under Hitler, a master of the "big lie."

human nature upon which those terrifyingly successful methods were based? These questions can be answered, for the most part, in Hitler's own words. And what remarkably clear and astute words they are! When he writes about such vast abstractions as Race and History and Providence, Hitler is strictly unreadable. But when he writes about the German masses and the methods he used for dominating and directing them, his style changes. Nonsense gives place to sense, bombast to a hard-boiled and cynical lucidity. In his philosophical lucubrations Hitler was either cloudily daydreaming or reproducing other people's half-baked notions. In his comments on crowds and propaganda he was writing of things he knew by firsthand experience. In the words of his ablest biographer, Mr. Alan Bullock, "Hitler was the greatest demagogue in history." Those who add, "only a demagogue," fail to appreciate the nature of political power in an age of mass politics. As he himself said, "To be a leader means to be able to move the masses." Hitler's aim was first to move the masses and then, having pried them loose from their traditional loyalties and moralities, to impose upon them (with the hypnotized consent of the majority) a new authoritarian order of his own devising. "Hitler," wrote Hermann Rauschning in 1939, "has a deep respect for the Catholic church and the Jesuit order; not because of their Christian doctrine, but because of the 'machinery' they have elaborated and controlled, their hierarchical system, their extremely clever tactics, their knowledge of human nature and their wise use of human weaknesses in ruling over believers." Ecclesiasticism without Christianity, the discipline of a monastic rule, not for God's sake or in order to achieve personal salvation, but for the sake of the State and for the greater glory and power of the demagogue turned Leader— 5 this was the goal toward which the systematic moving of the masses was to lead.

Let us see what Hitler thought of the masses he moved and how he did the moving. The first principle from which he started was a value judgment: the masses are utterly contemptible. They are incapable of abstract thinking and uninterested in any fact outside the circle of their immediate experience. Their behavior is determined, not by knowledge and reason, but by feelings and unconscious drives. It is in these drives and feelings that "the roots of their positive as well as their negative attitudes are implanted." To be successful a propagandist must learn how to manipulate these instincts and emotions. "The driving force which has brought about the most tremendous revolutions on this earth has never been a body of scientific teaching which has gained power over the masses, but always a devotion which has inspired them, and often a kind of hysteria which has urged them into action. Whoever wishes to win over the masses must know the key that will open the door of their hearts." . . . In post-Freudian jargon, of their unconscious.

Hitler made his strongest appeal to those members of the lower 6 middle classes who had been ruined by the inflation of 1923, and then ruined all over again by the depression of 1929 and the following years. "The masses" of whom he speaks were these bewildered, frustrated and chronically anxious millions. To make them more masslike, more homogeneously subhuman, he assembled them, by the thousands and the tens of thousands, in vast halls and arenas, where individuals could lose their personal identity, even their elementary humanity, and be merged with the crowd. A man or woman makes direct contact with society in two ways: as a member of some familial, professional or religious group, or as a member of a crowd. Groups are capable of being as moral and intelligent as the individuals who form them; a crowd is chaotic, has no purpose of its own and is capable of anything except intelligent action and realistic thinking. Assembled in a crowd, people lose their powers of reasoning and their capacity for moral choice. Their suggestibility is increased to the point where they cease to have any judgment or will of their own. They become very excitable, they lose all sense of individual or collective responsibility, they are subject to sudden accesses of rage, enthusiasm and panic. In a word, a man in a crowd behaves as though he had swallowed a large dose of some powerful intoxicant. He is a victim of what I have called "herd-poisoning." Like alcohol, herd-poison is an active, extraverted drug. The crowd-intoxicated individual escapes from responsibility, intelligence and morality into a kind of frantic, animal mindlessness.

During his long career as an agitator, Hitler had studied the 7 effects of herd-poison and had learned how to exploit them for his own purposes. He had discovered that the orator can appeal to those "hidden forces" which motivate men's actions, much more effectively than can the writer. Reading is a private, not a collective activity. The writer speaks only to individuals, sitting by themselves in a state of normal sobriety. The orator speaks to masses of individuals, already well primed with herd-poison. They are at his mercy and, if he knows his business, he can do what he likes with them. As an orator, Hitler knew his business supremely well. He was able, in his own words, "to follow the lead of the great mass in such a way that from the living emotion to his hearers the apt word which he needed would be suggested to him and in its turn this would go straight to the heart of his hearers." Otto Strasser called him a "loudspeaker, proclaiming the most secret desires, the least admissible instincts, the sufferings and personal revolts of a whole nation." Twenty years before Madison Avenue embarked upon "Motivational Research," Hitler was systematically exploring and exploiting the secret fears and hopes, the cravings, anxieties and frustrations of the German masses. It is by manipulating "hidden forces" that the advertising experts induce us to buy their wares—a toothpaste, a brand of cigarettes, a political candidate. And it is by appealing to the same hidden forces—and to others too dangerous for Madison Avenue to meddle with—that Hitler induced the German masses to buy themselves a Fuehrer, an insane philosophy and the Second World War.

Unlike the masses, intellectuals have a taste for rationality and an interest in facts. Their critical habit of mind makes them resistant to the kind of propaganda that works so well on the majority. Among the masses "instinct is supreme, and from instinct comes faith. . . . While the healthy common folk instinctively close their ranks to form a community of the people" (under a Leader, it goes without saying) "intellectuals run this way and that, like hens in a poultry yard. With them one cannot make history; they cannot be used as elements composing a community." Intellectuals are the kind of people who demand evidence and are shocked by logical inconsistencies and fallacies. They regard oversimplification as the original sin of the mind and have no use for the slogans, the unqualified assertions and sweeping generalizations which are the propagandist's stock in trade. "All effective propaganda," Hitler wrote, "must be confined to a few bare necessities and then must be expressed in a few stereotyped formulas." These stereotyped formulas must be constantly repeated, for "only constant repetition will finally succeed in imprinting an idea upon the memory of a crowd." Philosophy teaches us to feel uncertain about the things that seem to us self-evident. Propaganda, on the other hand, teaches us to accept as self-evident matters about which it would be reasonable to suspend our judgment or to feel doubt. The aim of the demagogue is to create social coherence under his own leadership. But, as Bertrand Russell has pointed out, "systems of dogma without empirical foundations, such as scholasticism, Marxism and fascism, have the advantage of producing a great deal of social coherence among their disciples." The demagogic propagandist must therefore be consistently dogmatic. All his statements are made without qualification. There are no grays in his picture of the world; everything is either diabolically black or celestially white. In Hitler's words, the propagandist should adopt "a systematically one-sided attitude towards every problem that has to be dealt with." He must never admit that he might be wrong or that people with a different point of view might be even partially right. Opponents should not be argued with; they should be attacked, shouted down, or, if they become too much of a nuisance, liquidated. The morally squeamish intellectual may be shocked by this kind of thing. But the masses are always convinced that "right is on the side of the active aggressor."

Such, then, was Hitler's opinion of humanity in the mass. It was 9 a very low opinion. Was it also an incorrect opinion? The tree is known by its fruits, and a theory of human nature which inspired the kind of techniques that proved so horribly effective must contain at least an element of truth. Virtue and intelligence belong to human beings as individuals freely associating with other individuals in small groups. So do sin and stupidity. But the subhuman mindlessness to which the demagogue makes his appeal, the moral imbecility on which he relies when he goads his victims into action, are characteristic not of men and women as individuals, but of men and women in masses. Mindlessness and moral idiocy are not characteristically human attributes; they are symptoms of herd-poisoning. In all the world's higher religions, salvation and enlightenment are for individuals. The kingdom of heaven is within the mind of a person, not within the collective mindlessness of a crowd. Christ promised to be present where two or three are gathered together. He did not say anything about being present where thousands are intoxicating one another with herd-poison. Under the Nazis enormous numbers of people were compelled to spend an enormous amount of time marching in serried ranks from point A to point B and back again to point A. "This keeping of the whole population on the march seemed to be a senseless waste of time and energy. Only much later," adds Hermann Rauschning, "was there revealed in it a subtle intention based on a well-judged adjustment of ends and means. Marching diverts men's thoughts. Marching kills thought. Marching makes an end of individuality. Marching is the indispensable magic stroke performed in order to accustom the people to a mechanical, quasi-ritualistic activity until it becomes second nature."

From his point of view and at the level where he had chosen 10 to do his dreadful work, Hitler was perfectly correct in his estimate of human nature. To those of us who look at men and women as individuals rather than as members of crowds, or of regimented collectives, he seems hideously wrong. In an age of accelerating overpopulation, of accelerating overorganization and even more efficient means of mass communication, how can we preserve the integrity and reassert the value of the human individual? This is a question that can still be asked and perhaps effectively answered. A generation from now it may be too late to find an answer and perhaps impossible, in the stifling collective climate of that future time, even to ask the question.

15 QUESTIONS ABOUT THE "LIBERAL MEDIA"

Jeff Cohen
Norman Solomon

One of the most enduring myths about the mainstream news [1] media is that they are "liberal." The myth flourishes to the extent that people don't ask pointed questions:

- If the news media are liberal, why have national dailies and newsweeklies regularly lauded those aspects of President Clinton's program that they view as "centrist" or "moderate," while questioning those viewed as liberal?

- If the news media are liberal, why is it that liberals are apt to be denigrated as ideologues, but status quo centrists or "moderates" are presented as free of ideological baggage?

- If the news media are liberal, why did most outlets praise Clinton's selection of David Gergen, who advocated Reagan policies, while pillorying civil rights lawyer Lani Guinier?

- If the news media are liberal, why did they applaud conservative White House appointees like Lloyd Bentsen and Les Aspin, while challenging liberals like Donna Shalala, Johnetta Cole and Roberta Achtenberg?

It also helps to look back at history and ask questions: [2]

- If the news media are liberal, why have Clinton's meager tax hikes on the wealthy been referred to as "soaking the rich" or "class warfare," but President Reagan's giveaways to the wealthy were euphemized as "tax reform"?

- If the news media are liberal, why have national outlets been far tougher in scrutinizing Democratic presidents Carter and Clinton than Republicans Reagan and Bush?

- If the news media are liberal, why have they buried important facts, such as the shrinking of corporate income tax from 25 percent of federal expenditures in the 1960s to only about 8 percent today?

- If the news media are liberal, why have they given short shrift to reform proposals—tax-financed national health insurance, federally-supported child care, government jobs programs—that their own polls show are overwhelmingly popular with the public?

Pundits and commentators have gained increasing prominence in the 3 *media, often eclipsing the reporters:*

- If the news media are liberal, why were the first two political pundits to appear on national TV every day of the week both conservatives: Patrick Buchanan and John McLaughlin? Was it their good looks?

- If the news media are liberal, why does the media spectrum typically extend from unabashed right-wingers to tepid centrists who go to great lengths—attacking progressive ideas and individuals—to prove they're not left-wing? Why do pundit debates on national TV have *Wall Street Journal* reporters representing "the left"?

- If the news media are liberal, why are TV pundit programs— even on "public television"—sponsored by conservative businesses like General Electric, Pepsico and Archer Daniels Midland?

- If the news media are liberal, why was Rush Limbaugh the first host in the history of American television to be allowed to use his national politics show to campaign day after day for a presidential candidate?

- If the news media are liberal, why do right-wing hosts usually dominate talk radio—even in liberal cities?

- If the news media are liberal, why are there dozens of widely syndicated columnists who champion corporate interests, but few who champion consumer or labor rights?

In analyzing the bias of any institution, it helps to look at who owns it. 4 *Which leads to a final question:*

- If the news media are liberal, why are they owned and sponsored by big corporations that spend millions of dollars to lobby *against* liberal measures in Washington?

TELEVISION: THE PLUG-IN DRUG

Marie Winn

Not much more than fifty years after the introduction of televi- 1
sion into American society, the medium has become so deeply
ingrained in daily life that in many states the TV set has attained the
rank of a legal necessity, safe from repossession in case of debt along
with clothes and cooking utensils. Only in the early years after television's introduction did writers and commentators have sufficient
perspective to separate the activity of watching television from the
actual content it offers the viewer. In those days writers frequently
discussed the effects of television on family life. However, a curious
myopia afflicted those first observers: almost without exception they
regarded television as a favorable, beneficial, indeed, wondrous
influence upon the family.

"Television is going to be a real asset in every home where there 2
are children," predicted a writer in 1949.

"Television will take over your way of living and change your 3
children's habits, but this change can be a wonderful improvement,"
claimed another commentator.

"No survey's needed, of course, to establish that television has 4
brought the family together in one room," wrote the *New York Times*'s
television critic in 1949.

The early articles about television were almost invariably accom- 5
panied by a photograph or illustration showing a family cozily sitting together before the television set, Sis on Mom's lap, Buddy
perched on the arm of Dad's chair, Dad with his arm around Mom's
shoulder. Who could have guessed that twenty or so years later Mom
would be watching a drama in the kitchen, the kids would be looking at cartoons in their room, while Dad would be taking in the ball
game in the living room?

Of course television sets were enormously expensive when they 6
first came on the market. The idea that by the year 2000 more than
three quarters of all American families would own two or more sets
would have seemed preposterous. The splintering of the multiple-set
family was something the early writers did not foresee. Nor did anyone imagine the number of hours children would eventually devote
to television, the changes television would effect upon child-rearing
methods, the increasing domination of family schedules by chil-

dren's viewing requirements—in short, the power of television to dominate family life.

As children's consumption of the new medium increased 7 together with parental concern about the possible effects of so much television viewing, a steady refrain helped soothe and reassure anxious parents. "Television always enters a pattern of influences that already exist: the home, the peer group, the school, the church and culture generally," wrote the authors of an early and influential study of television's effects on children. In other words, if the child's home life is all right, parents need not worry about the effects of too much television watching.

But television did not merely influence the child; it deeply influ- 8 enced that "pattern of influences" everyone hoped would ameliorate the new medium's effects. Home and family life have changed in important ways since the advent of television. The peer group has become television-oriented, and much of the time children spend together is occupied by television viewing. Culture generally has been transformed by television. Participation in church and community activities has diminished, with television a primary cause of this change. Therefore it is improper to assign to television the subsidiary role its many apologists insist it plays. Television is not merely one of a number of important influences upon today's child. Through the changes it has made in family life, television emerges as *the* important influence in children's lives today.

The Quality of Life

Television's contribution to family life has been an equivocal one. 9 For while it has, indeed, kept the members of the family from dispersing, it has not served to bring them together. By its domination of the time families spend together, it destroys the special quality that distinguishes one family from another, a quality that depends to a great extent on what a family does, what special rituals, games, recurrent jokes, familiar songs, and shared activities it accumulates.

Yet parents have accepted a television-dominated family life so 10 completely that they cannot see how the medium is involved in whatever problems they might be having. A first-grade teacher reports:

I have one child in the group who's an only child. I wanted to find out more about her family life because this little girl was quite isolated from the group, didn't make friends, so I talked to her mother. Well, they don't have time to do anything in the evening, the mother said. The parents come home after picking up the child at the baby-sitter's. Then the mother fixes dinner while the child watches TV. Then they have dinner and the child goes to bed. I said to this mother. "Well, couldn't she help you fix dinner? That would be a nice time for the two of you to talk," and the mother said, "Oh, but I'd hate to have her miss *Zoom*. It's such a good program!"

Several decades ago a writer and mother of two boys aged three 11 and seven described her family's television schedule in a newspaper article. Though some of the programs her kids watched then have changed, the situation she describes remains the same for great numbers of families today:

> We were in the midst of a full-scale War. Every day was a new battle and every program was a major skirmish. We agreed it was a bad scene all around and were ready to enter diplomatic negotiations. . . . In principle we have agreed on 2½ hours of TV a day, *Sesame Street*, *Electric Company* (with dinner gobbled up in between) and two half-hour shows between 7 and 8:30, which enables the grown-ups to eat in peace and prevents the two boys from destroying one another. Their pre-bedtime choice is dreadful, because, as Josh recently admitted, "There's nothing much on I really like." So . . . it's *What's My Line* or *To Tell the Truth*. . . . Clearly there is a need for first-rate children's shows at this time. . . .

Consider the "family life" described here: Presumably the father 12 comes home from work during the *Sesame Street–Electric Company* stint. The children are either watching television, gobbling their dinner, or both. While the parents eat their dinner in peaceful privacy, the children watch another hour of television. Then there is only a half-hour left before bedtime, just enough time for baths, getting pajamas on, brushing teeth, and so on. The children's evening is regimented with an almost military precision. They watch their favorite programs, and when there is "nothing much on I really like," they watch whatever else is on—because *watching* is the important thing. Their mother does not see anything amiss with watching programs just for the sake of watching; she only wishes there were some first-rate children's shows on at those times.

Without conjuring up fantasies of bygone eras with family games 13 and long, leisurely meals, the question arises: isn't there a better family life available than this dismal, mechanized arrangement of children watching television for however long is allowed them, evening after evening?

Of course, families today still do things together at times: go 14 camping in the summer, go to the zoo on a nice Sunday, take various trips and expeditions. But their ordinary daily life together is diminished—those hours of sitting around at the dinner table, the spontaneous taking up of an activity, the little games invented by children on the spur of the moment when there is nothing else to do, the scribbling, the chatting, and even the quarreling, all the things that form the fabric of a family, that define a childhood. Instead, the children have their regular schedule of television programs and bedtime, and the parents have their peaceful dinner together.

The author of the quoted newspaper article notes that "keeping 15 a family sane means mediating between the needs of both children and adults." But surely the needs of the adults in that family were being better met than the needs of the children. The kids were effectively shunted away and rendered untroublesome, while their parents enjoyed a life as undemanding as that of any childless couple. In reality, it is those very demands that young children make upon a family that lead to growth, and it is the way parents respond to those demands that builds the relationships upon which the future of the family depends. If the family does not accumulate its backlog of shared experiences, shared everyday experiences that occur and recur and change and develop, then it is not likely to survive as anything other than a caretaking institution.

Family Rituals

Ritual is defined by sociologists as "that part of family life that 16 the family likes about itself, is proud of and wants formally to continue." Another text notes that "the development of a ritual by a family is an index of the common interest of its members in the family as a group."

What has happened to family rituals, those regular, dependable, 17 recurrent happenings that gave members of a family a feeling of belonging to a home rather than living in it merely for the sake of convenience, those experiences that act as the adhesive of family unity far more than any material advantages?

Mealtime rituals, going-to-bed rituals, illness rituals, holiday 18 rituals—how many of these have survived the inroads of the television set?

A young woman who grew up near Chicago reminisces about 19
her childhood and gives an idea of the effects of television upon family rituals:

> As a child I had millions of relatives around—my parents both
> come from relatively large families. My father had nine brothers
> and sisters. And so every holiday there was this great swoop-down
> of aunts, uncles, and millions of cousins. I just remember how
> wonderful it used to be. These thousands of cousins would come
> and everyone would play and ultimately, after dinner, all the
> women would be in the front of the house, drinking coffee and
> talking, all the men would be in the back of the house, drinking
> and smoking, and all the kids would be all over the place, playing
> hide and seek. Christmas time was particularly nice because every-
> one always brought all their toys and games. Our house had a cou-
> ple of rooms with go-through closets, so there were always kids
> running in a great circle route. I remember it was just wonderful.
> And then all of a sudden one year I remember becoming sud-
> denly aware of how different everything had become. The kids
> were no longer playing Monopoly or Clue or the other games we
> used to play together. It was because we had a television set which
> had been turned on for a football game. All of that socializing that
> had gone on previously had ended. Now everyone was sitting in
> front of the television set, on a holiday, at a family party! I remem-
> ber being stunned by how awful that was. Somehow the television
> had become more attractive.

As families have come to spend more and more of their time 20
together engaged in the single activity of television watching, those
rituals and pastimes that once gave family life its special quality have
become more and more uncommon. Not since prehistoric times,
when cave families hunted, gathered, ate, and slept, with little time
remaining to accumulate a culture of any significance, have families
been reduced to such a sameness.

Real People

The relationships of family members to each other are affected by 21
television's powerful competition in both obvious and subtle ways.
For surely the hours that children spend in a one-way relationship
with television people, an involvement that allows for no communication or interaction, must have some effect on their relationships
with real-life people.

Studies show the importance of eye-to-eye contact, for instance, 22 in real-life relationships, and indicate that the nature of one's eye-contact patterns, whether one looks another squarely in the eye or looks to the side or shifts one's gaze from side to side, may play a significant role in one's success or failure in human relationships. But no eye contact is possible in the child-television relationship, although in certain children's programs people purport to speak directly to the child and the camera fosters this illusion by focusing directly upon the person being filmed. How might such a distortion affect a child's development of trust, of openness, of an ability to relate well to *real* people?

Bruno Bettelheim suggested an answer: 23

> Children who have been taught, or conditioned, to listen passively most of the day to the warm verbal communications coming from the TV screen, to the deep emotional appeal of the so-called TV personality, are often unable to respond to real persons because they arouse so much less feeling than the skilled actor. Worse, they lose the ability to learn from reality because life experiences are much more complicated than the ones they see on the screen. . . .

A teacher makes a similar observation about her personal view- 24 ing experiences:

> I have trouble mobilizing myself and dealing with real people after watching a few hours of television. It's just hard to make that transition from watching television to a real relationship. I suppose it's because there was no effort necessary while I was watching, and dealing with real people always requires a bit of effort. Imagine, then, how much harder it might be to do the same thing for a small child, particularly one who watches a lot of television every day.

But more obviously damaging to family relationships is the elim- 25 ination of opportunities to talk and converse, or to argue, to air grievances between parents and children and brothers and sisters. Families frequently use television to avoid confronting their problems, problems that will not go away if they are ignored but will only fester and become less easily resolvable as time goes on.

A mother reports: 26

> I find myself, with three children, wanting to turn on the TV set when they're fighting. I really have to struggle not to do it because I feel that's telling them this is the solution to the quarrel—but it's so tempting that I often do it.

A family therapist discusses the use of television as an avoidance   27
mechanism:

> In a family I know the father comes home from work and turns on
> the television set. The children come and watch with him and the
> wife serves them their meal in front of the set. He then goes and
> takes a shower, or works on the car or something. She then goes
> and has her own dinner in front of the television set. It's a symp-
> tom of a deeper-rooted problem, sure. But it would help them all
> to get rid of the set. It would be far easier to work on what the
> symptom really means without the television. The television sim-
> ply encourages a double avoidance of each other. They'd find out
> more quickly what was going on if they weren't able to hide
> behind the TV. Things wouldn't necessarily be better, of course, but
> they wouldn't be anesthetized.

A number of research studies done when television was a rela-   28
tively new medium demonstrated that television interfered with
family activities and the formation of family relationships. One
survey showed that 78 percent of the respondents indicated no
conversation taking place during viewing except at specified times
such as commercials. The study noted: "The television atmosphere in
most households is one of quiet absorption on the part of family
members who are present. The nature of the family social life during
a program could be described as 'parallel' rather than interactive,
and the set does seem to dominate family life when it is on." Thirty-
six percent of the respondents in another study indicated that television viewing was the only family activity participated in during the
week.

The situation has only worsened during the intervening decades.   29
When the studies were made, the great majority of American families
had only one television set. Though the family may have spent more
time watching TV in those early days, at least they were all together
while they watched. Today the vast majority of all families have two
or more sets, and nearly a third of all children live in homes with
four or more TVs. The most telling statistic: almost 60 percent of
all families watch television during meals, and not necessarily at
the same TV set. When do they talk about what they did that day?
When do they make plans, exchange views, share jokes, tell about
their triumphs or little disasters? When do they get to be a real
family?

Undermining the Family

Of course television has not been the only factor in the decline   30
of family life in America. The steadily rising divorce rate, the increase
in the number of working mothers, the trends towards people
moving far away from home, the breakdown of neighborhoods and
communities—all these have seriously affected the family.

Obviously the sources of family breakdown do not necessarily   31
come from the family itself, but from the circumstances in which the
family finds itself and the way of life imposed upon it by those circumstances. As Urie Bronfenbrenner has suggested:

> When those circumstances and the way of life they generate under-
> mine relationships of trust and emotional security between family
> members, when they make it difficult for parents to care for, edu-
> cate, and enjoy their children, when there is no support or recog-
> nition from the outside world for one's role as a parent, and when
> time spent with one's family means frustration of career, personal
> fulfillment, and peace of mind, then the development of the child
> is adversely affected.

Certainly television is not the single destroyer of American fam-   32
ily life. But the medium's dominant role in the family serves to anes-
thetize parents into accepting their family's diminished state and
prevents them from struggling to regain some of the richness the
family once possessed.

One research study alone seems to contradict the idea that televi-   33
sion has a negative impact on family life. In their important book
Television and the Quality of Life, sociologists Robert Kubey and Mihaly
Csikszentmihalyi observe that the heaviest viewers of TV among their
subjects were "no less likely to spend time with their families" than the
lightest viewers. Moreover, those heavy viewers reported feeling hap-
pier, more relaxed, and satisfied when watching TV with their families
than light viewers did. Based on these reports, the researchers reached
the conclusion that "television viewing harmonizes with family life."

Using the same data, however, the researchers made another   34
observation about the heavy and light viewers: ". . . families that
spend substantial portions of their time together watching television
are likely to experience greater percentages of their family time feeling relatively passive and unchallenged compared with families who
spend small proportions of their time watching TV."

At first glance the two observations seem at odds: the heavier 35
viewers feel happy and satisfied, yet their family time is more passive and unchallenging—less satisfying in reality. But when one considers the nature of the television experience, the contradiction
vanishes. Surely it stands to reason that the television experience is
instrumental in preventing viewers from recognizing its dulling
effects, much as a mind-altering drug might do.

In spite of everything, the American family muddles on, dimly 36
aware that something is amiss but distracted from an understanding
of its plight by an endless stream of television images. As family ties
grow weaker and vaguer, as children's lives become more separate
from their parents', as parents' educational role in their children's
lives is taken over by the media, the school, and the peer group, family life becomes increasingly more unsatisfying for both parents and
children. All that seems to be left is love, an abstraction that family
members know is necessary but find great difficulty giving to each
other since the traditional opportunities for expressing it within the
family have been reduced or eliminated.

THE COOLHUNT

Malcolm Gladwell

Who decides what's cool? Certain kids in certain places—and only the coolhunters know who they are. [1]

1.

Baysie Wightman met DeeDee Gordon, appropriately enough, on a [2] coolhunt. It was 1992. Baysie was a big shot for Converse, and DeeDee, who was barely twenty-one, was running a very cool boutique called Placid Planet, on Newbury Street in Boston. Baysie came in with a camera crew—one she often used when she was coolhunting—and said, "I've been watching your store, I've seen you, I've heard you know what's up," because it was Baysie's job at Converse to find people who knew what was up and she thought DeeDee was one of those people. DeeDee says that she responded with reserve—that "I was like, 'Whatever.'"—but Baysie said that if DeeDee ever wanted to come and work at Converse she should just call, and nine months later DeeDee called. This was about the time the cool kids had decided they didn't want the hundred-and-twenty-five-dollar basketball sneaker with seventeen different kinds of high-technology materials and colors and air-cushioned heels anymore. They wanted simplicity and authenticity, and Baysie picked up on that. She brought back the Converse One Star, which was a vulcanized, suede, low-top classic old-school sneaker from the nineteen-seventies, and, sure enough, the One Star quickly became the signature shoe of the retro era. Remember what Kurt Cobain was wearing in the famous picture of him lying dead on the ground after committing suicide? Black Converse One Stars. DeeDee's big score was calling the sandal craze. She had been out in Los Angeles and had kept seeing the white teen-age girls dressing up like cholos, Mexican gangsters, in tight white tank tops known as "wife beaters," with a bra strap hanging out, and long shorts and tube socks and shower sandals. DeeDee recalls, "I'm like, 'I'm telling you, Baysie, this is going to hit. There are just too many people wearing it. We have to make a shower sandal.'" So Baysie, DeeDee, and a designer came up with the idea of making a retro sneaker-sandal, cutting the back off the One Star and putting a thick outsole on it. It was huge, and, amazingly, it's still huge.

Today, Baysie works for Reebok as general-merchandise 3
manager—part of the team trying to return Reebok to the position it
enjoyed in the mid-nineteen-eighties as the country's hottest sneaker
company. DeeDee works for an advertising agency in Del Mar called
Lambesis, where she puts out a quarterly tip sheet called the L Report
on what the cool kids in major American cities are thinking and
doing and buying. Baysie and DeeDee are best friends. They talk on
the phone all the time.

They get together whenever Baysie is in L.A. (DeeDee: "It's, like, 4
how many times can you drive past O.J. Simpson's house?"), and
between them they can talk for hours about the art of the coolhunt.
They're the Lewis and Clark of cool.

What they have is what everybody seems to want these days, 5
which is a window on the world of the street. Once, when fashion
trends were set by the big couture houses—when cool was trickle-
down—that wasn't important. But sometime in the past few decades
things got turned over, and fashion became trickle-up. It's now about
chase and flight—designers and retailers and the mass consumer giving chase to the elusive prey of street cool—and the rise of coolhunting as a profession shows how serious the chase has become. The
sneakers of Nike and Reebok used to come out yearly. Now a new
style comes out every season. Apparel designers used to have an
eighteen-month lead time between concept and sale. Now they're
reducing that to a year, or even six months, in order to react faster to
new ideas from the street. The paradox, of course, is that the better
coolhunters become at bringing the mainstream close to the cutting
edge, the more elusive the cutting edge becomes. This is the first rule
of the cool: The quicker the chase, the quicker the flight. The act of
discovering what's cool is what causes cool to move on, which
explains the triumphant circularity of coolhunting: because we have
coolhunters like DeeDee and Baysie, cool changes more quickly, and
because cool changes more quickly, we need coolhunters like DeeDee
and Baysie.

DeeDee is tall and glamorous, with short hair she has dyed so 6
often that she claims to have forgotten her real color. She drives a yellow 1977 Trans Am with a burgundy stripe down the center and a
1973 Mercedes 450 SL, and lives in a spare, Japanese-style cabin in
Laurel Canyon. She uses words like "rad" and "totally," and offers
non-stop, deadpan pronouncements on pop culture, as in "It's all
about Pee-wee Herman." She sounds at first like a teen, like the same
teens who, at Lambesis, it is her job to follow. But teen speech—
particularly girl-teen speech, with its fixation on reported speech ("so

she goes," "and I'm like," "and he goes") and its stock vocabulary of accompanying grimaces and gestures—is about using language less to communicate than to fit in. DeeDee uses teen speech to set herself apart, and the result is, for lack of a better word, really cool. She doesn't do the teen thing of climbing half an octave at the end of every sentence. Instead, she drags out her vowels for emphasis, so that if she mildly disagreed with something I'd said she would say "Maalcolm" and if she strongly disagreed with what I'd said she would say "Maaalcolm."

Baysie is older, just past forty (although you would never guess that), and went to Exeter and Middlebury and had two grandfathers who went to Harvard (although you wouldn't guess that, either). She has curly brown hair and big green eyes and long legs and so much energy that it is hard to imagine her asleep, or resting, or even standing still for longer than thirty seconds. The hunt for cool is an obsession with her, and DeeDee is the same way. DeeDee used to sit on the corner of West Broadway and Prince in SoHo—back when SoHo was cool—and take pictures of everyone who walked by for an entire hour. Baysie can tell you precisely where she goes on her Reebok coolhunts to find the really cool alternative white kids ("I'd maybe go to Portland and hang out where the skateboarders hang out near that bridge") or which snowboarding mountain has cooler kids—Stratton, in Vermont, or Summit County, in Colorado. (Summit, definitely.) DeeDee can tell you on the basis of the L Report's research exactly how far Dallas is behind New York in coolness (from six to eight months). Baysie is convinced that Los Angeles is not happening right now: "In the early nineteen-nineties a lot more was coming from L.A. They had a big trend with the whole Melrose Avenue look—the stupid goatees, the shorter hair. It was cleaned-up after-grunge. There were a lot of places you could go to buy vinyl records. It was a strong place to go for looks. Then it went back to being horrible." DeeDee is convinced that Japan is happening: "I linked onto this future-technology thing two years ago. Now look at it, it's huge. It's the whole resurgence of Nike—Nike being larger than life. I went to Japan and saw the kids just bailing the most technologically advanced Nikes with their little dresses and little outfits and I'm like, 'Whoa, this is trippy!' It's performance mixed with fashion. It's really superheavy." Baysie has a theory that Liverpool is cool right now because it's the birthplace of the whole "lad" look, which involves soccer blokes in the pubs going superdressy and wearing Dolce & Gabbana and Polo Sport and Reebok Classics on their feet. But when

7

I asked DeeDee about that, she just rolled her eyes: "Sometimes Baysie goes off on these tangents. Man, I love that woman!"

I used to think that if I talked to Baysie and DeeDee long enough 8 I could write a coolhunting manual, an encyclopedia of cool. But then I realized that the manual would have so many footnotes and caveats that it would be unreadable. Coolhunting is not about the articulation of a coherent philosophy of cool. It's just a collection of spontaneous observations and predictions that differ from one moment to the next and from one coolhunter to the next. Ask a coolhunter where the baggy-jeans look came from, for example, and you might get any number of answers: urban black kids mimicking the jailhouse look, skateboarders looking for room to move, snowboarders trying not to look like skiers, or, alternatively, all three at once, in some grand concordance.

Or take the question of exactly how Tommy Hilfiger—a forty- 9 five-year-old white guy from Greenwich, Connecticut, doing all-American preppy clothes—came to be the designer of choice for urban black America. Some say it was all about the early and visible endorsement given Hilfiger by the hip-hop auteur Grand Puba, who wore a dark-green-and-blue Tommy jacket over a white Tommy T-shirt as he leaned on his black Lamborghini on the cover of the hugely influential "Grand Puba 2000" CD, and whose love for Hilfiger soon spread to other rappers. (Who could forget the rhymes of Mobb Deep? "Tommy was my nigga / And couldn't figure / How me and Hilfiger / used to move through with vigor.") Then I had lunch with one of Hilfiger's designers, a twenty-six-year-old named Ulrich (Ubi) Simpson, who has a Puerto Rican mother and a Dutch-Venezuelan father, plays lacrosse, snowboards, surfs the long board, goes to hip-hop concerts, listens to Jungle, Edith Piaf, opera, rap, and Metallica, and has working with him on his design team a twenty-seven-year-old black guy from Montclair with dreadlocks, a twenty-two-year-old Asian-American who lives on the Lower East Side, a twenty-five-year-old South Asian guy from Fiji, and a twenty-one-year-old white graffiti artist from Queens. That's when it occurred to me that maybe the reason Tommy Hilfiger can make white culture cool to black culture is that he has people working for him who are cool in both cultures simultaneously. Then again, maybe it was all Grand Puba. Who knows?

One day last month, Baysie took me on a coolhunt to the Bronx 10 and Harlem, lugging a big black canvas bag with twenty-four different shoes that Reebok is about to bring out, and as we drove down

Fordham Road, she had her head out the window like a little kid, checking out what everyone on the street was wearing. We went to Dr. Jay's, which is the cool place to buy sneakers in the Bronx, and Baysie crouched down on the floor and started pulling the shoes out of her bag one by one, soliciting opinions from customers who gathered around and asking one question after another, in rapid sequence. One guy she listened closely to was maybe eighteen or nineteen, with a diamond stud in his ear and a thin beard. He was wearing a Polo baseball cap, a brown leather jacket, and the big, oversized leather boots that are everywhere uptown right now. Baysie would hand him a shoe and he would hold it, look at the top, and move it up and down and flip it over. The first one he didn't like: "Oh-kay." The second one he hated: he made a growling sound in his throat even before Baysie could give it to him, as if to say, "Put it back in the bag—now!" But when she handed him a new DMX RXT—a low-cut run/walk shoe in white and blue and mesh with a translucent "ice" sole, which retails for a hundred and ten dollars—he looked at it long and hard and shook his head in pure admiration and just said two words, dragging each of them out: "No doubt."

Baysie was interested in what he was saying, because the DMX 11 RXT she had was a girls' shoe that actually hadn't been doing all that well. Later, she explained to me that the fact that the boys loved the shoe was critical news, because it suggested that Reebok had a potential hit if it just switched the shoe to the men's section. How she managed to distill this piece of information from the crowd of teenagers around her, how she made any sense of the two dozen shoes in her bag, most of which (to my eyes, anyway) looked pretty much the same, and how she knew which of the teens to really focus on was a mystery. Baysie is a Wasp from New England, and she crouched on the floor in Dr. Jay's for almost an hour, talking and joking with the homeboys without a trace of condescension or self-consciousness.

Near the end of her visit, a young boy walked up and sat down 12 on the bench next to her. He was wearing a black woolen cap with white stripes pulled low, a blue North Face pleated down jacket, a pair of baggy Guess jeans, and, on his feet, Nike Air Jordans. He couldn't have been more than thirteen. But when he started talking you could see Baysie's eyes light up, because somehow she knew the kid was the real thing.

"How many pairs of shoes do you buy a month?" Baysie asked. 13

"Two," the kid answered. "And if at the end I find one more I like 14 I get to buy that, too."

Baysie was onto him. "Does your mother spoil you?" 15

The kid blushed, but a friend next to him was laughing. 16
"Whatever he wants, he gets."

Baysie laughed, too. She had the DMX RXT in his size. He tried 17
them on. He rocked back and forth, testing them. He looked back at
Baysie. He was dead serious now: "Make sure these come out."

Baysie handed him the new "Rush" Emmitt Smith shoe due out 18
in the fall. One of the boys had already pronounced it "phat," and
another had looked through the marbleized-foam cradle in the heel
and cried out in delight, "This is bug!" But this kid was the acid test,
because this kid knew cool. He paused. He looked at it hard.
"Reebok," he said, soberly and carefully, "is trying to get butter."

In the car on the way back to Manhattan, Baysie repeated it 19
twice. "Not better. Butter! That kid could totally tell you what he
thinks." Baysie had spent an hour coolhunting in a shoe store and
found out that Reebok's efforts were winning the highest of hip-hop
praise. "He was so fucking smart."

2.

If you want to understand how trends work, and why coolhunters 20
like Baysie and DeeDee have become so important, a good place to
start is with what's known as diffusion research, which is the study
of how ideas and innovations spread. Diffusion researchers do things
like spending five years studying the adoption of irrigation techniques in a Colombian mountain village, or developing complex
matrices to map the spread of new math in the Pittsburgh school system. What they do may seem like a far cry from, say, how the Tommy
Hilfiger thing spread from Harlem to every suburban mall in the
country, but it really isn't: both are about how new ideas spread from
one person to the next.

One of the most famous diffusion studies is Bruce Ryan and Neal 21
Gross's analysis of the spread of hybrid seed corn in Greene County,
Iowa, in the nineteen-thirties. The new seed corn was introduced
there in about 1928, and it was superior in every respect to the seed
that had been used by farmers for decades. But it wasn't adopted all
at once. Of two hundred and fifty-nine farmers studied by Ryan and
Gross, only a handful had started planting the new seed by 1933. In
1934, sixteen took the plunge. In 1935, twenty-one more followed; the
next year, there were thirty-six, and the year after that a whopping

sixty-one. The succeeding figures were then forty-six, thirty-six, four-teen, and three, until, by 1941, all but two of the two hundred and fifty-nine farmers studied were using the new seed. In the language of diffusion research, the handful of farmers who started trying hybrid seed corn at the very beginning of the thirties were the "inno-vators," the adventurous ones. The slightly larger group that fol-lowed them was the "early adopters." They were the opinion leaders in the community, the respected, thoughtful people who watched and analyzed what those wild innovators were doing and then did it themselves. Then came the big bulge of farmers in 1936, 1937, and 1938—the "early majority" and the "late majority," which is to say the deliberate and the skeptical masses, who would never try any-thing until the most respected farmers had tried it. Only after they had been converted did the "laggards," the most traditional of all, follow suit. The critical thing about this sequence is that it is almost entirely interpersonal. According to Ryan and Gross, only the inno-vators relied to any great extent on radio advertising and farm jour-nals and seed salesmen in making their decision to switch to the hybrid. Everyone else made his decision overwhelmingly because of the example and the opinions of his neighbors and peers.

Isn't this just how fashion works? A few years ago, the classic 22 brushed-suede Hush Puppies with the lightweight crepe sole—the moc-toe oxford known as the Duke and the slip-on with the golden buckle known as the Columbia—were selling barely sixty-five thou-sand pairs a year. The company was trying to walk away from the whole suede casual look entirely. It wanted to do "aspirational" shoes: "active casuals" in smooth leather, like the Mall Walker, with a Comfort Curve technology outsole and a heel stabilizer—the kind of shoes you see in Kinney's for $39.95. But then something strange started happening. Two Hush Puppies executives—Owen Baxter and Jeff Lewis—were doing a fashion shoot for their Mall Walkers and ran into a creative consultant from Manhattan named Jeffrey Miller, who informed them that the Dukes and the Columbias weren't dead, they were dead chic. "We were being told," Baxter recalls, "that there were areas in the Village, in SoHo, where the shoes were selling—in resale shops—and that people were wearing the old Hush Puppies. They were going to the ma-and-pa stores, the little stores that still carried them, and there was this authenticity of being able to say, 'I am wearing an original pair of Hush Puppies.'"

Baxter and Lewis—tall, solid, fair-haired Midwestern guys with 23 thick, shiny wedding bands—are shoe men, first and foremost.

Baxter was working the cash register at his father's shoe store in Mount Prospect, Illinois, at the age of thirteen. Lewis was doing inventory in his father's shoe store in Pontiac, Michigan, at the age of seven. Baxter was in the National Guard during the 1968 Democratic Convention, in Chicago, and was stationed across the street from the Conrad Hilton downtown, right in the middle of things. Today, the two men work out of Rockford, Michigan (population thirty-eight hundred), where Hush Puppies has been making the Dukes and the Columbias in an old factory down by the Rogue River for almost forty years. They took me to the plant when I was in Rockford. In a crowded, noisy, low-slung building, factory workers stand in long rows, gluing, stapling, and sewing together shoes in dozens of bright colors, and the two executives stopped at each production station and described it in detail. Lewis and Baxter know shoes. But they would be the first to admit that they don't know cool. "Miller was saying that there is something going on with the shoes—that Isaac Mizrahi was wearing the shoes for his personal use," Lewis told me. We were seated around the conference table in the Hush Puppies headquarters in Rockford, with the snow and the trees outside and a big water tower behind us. "I think it's fair to say that at the time we had no idea who Isaac Mizrahi was."

By late 1994, things had begun to happen in a rush. First, the 24 designer John Bartlett called. He wanted to use Hush Puppies as accessories in his spring collection. Then Anna Sui called. Miller, the man from Manhattan, flew out to Michigan to give advice on a new line ("Of course, packing my own food and thinking about 'Fargo' in the corner of my mind"). A few months later, in Los Angeles, the designer Joel Fitzpatrick put a twenty-five-foot inflatable basset hound on the roof of his store on La Brea Avenue and gutted his adjoining art gallery to turn it into a Hush Puppies department, and even before he opened—while he was still painting and putting up shelves—Pee-wee Herman walked in and asked for a couple of pairs. Pee-wee Herman! "It was total word of mouth. I didn't even have a sign back then," Fitzpatrick recalls. In 1995, the company sold four hundred and thirty thousand pairs of the classic Hush Puppies. In 1996, it sold a million six hundred thousand, and that was only scratching the surface, because in Europe and the rest of the world, where Hush Puppies have a huge following—where they might out-sell the American market four to one—the revival was just beginning.

The cool kids who started wearing old Dukes and Columbias 25 from thrift shops were the innovators. Pee-wee Herman, wandering in off the street, was an early adopter. The million six hundred thousand people who bought Hush Puppies last year are the early majority, jumping in because the really cool people have already blazed the trail. Hush Puppies are moving through the country just the way hybrid seed corn moved through Greene County—all of which illustrates what coolhunters can and cannot do. If Jeffrey Miller had been wrong—if cool people hadn't been digging through the thrift shops for Hush Puppies—and he had arbitrarily decided that Baxter and Lewis should try to convince non-cool people that the shoes were cool, it wouldn't have worked. You can't convince the late majority that Hush Puppies are cool, because the late majority makes its coolness decisions on the basis of what the early majority is doing, and you can't convince the early majority, because the early majority is looking at the early adopters, and you can't convince the early adopters, because they take their cues from the innovators. The innovators do get their cool ideas from people other than their peers, but the fact is that they are the last people who can be convinced by a marketing campaign that a pair of suede shoes is cool. These are, after all, the people who spent hours sifting through thrift-store bins. And why did they do that? Because their definition of cool is doing something that nobody else is doing. A company can intervene in the cool cycle. It can put its shoes on really cool celebrities and on fashion runways and on MTV. It can accelerate the transition from the innovator to the early adopter and on to the early majority. But it can't just manufacture cool out of thin air, and that's the second rule of cool.

At the peak of the Hush Puppies craziness last year, Hush   ₂₆
Puppies won the prize for best accessory at the Council of Fashion Designers' awards dinner, at Lincoln Center. The award was accepted by the Hush Puppies president, Louis Dubrow, who came out wearing a pair of custom-made black patent-leather Hush Puppies and stood there blinking and looking at the assembled crowd as if it were the last scene of "Close Encounters of the Third Kind." It was a strange moment. There was the president of the Hush Puppies company, of Rockford, Michigan, population thirty-eight hundred, sharing a stage with Calvin Klein and Donna Karan and Isaac Mizrahi—and all because some kids in the East Village began combing through thrift shops for old Dukes. Fashion was at the mercy of those kids, whoever they were, and it was a wonderful thing if the kids picked you, but a scary thing, too, because it meant that cool was something you could not control. You needed someone to find cool and tell you what it was.

3.

When Baysie Wightman went to Dr. Jay's, she was looking for cus- 27
tomer response to the new shoes Reebok had planned for the fourth
quarter of 1997 and the first quarter of 1998. This kind of customer
testing is critical at Reebok, because the last decade has not been kind
to the company. In 1987, it had a third of the American athletic-shoe
market, well ahead of Nike. Last year, it had sixteen per cent. "The
kid in the store would say, 'I'd like this shoe if your logo wasn't on
it,'" E. Scott Morris, who's a senior designer for Reebok, told me.
"That's kind of a punch in the mouth. But we've all seen it. You go
into a shoe store. The kid picks up the shoe and says, 'Ah, man, this
is nice.' He turns the shoe around and around. He looks at it under-
neath. He looks at the side and he goes, 'Ah, this is Reebok,' and says,
'I ain't buying this,' and puts the shoe down and walks out. And you
go, 'You was just digging it a minute ago. What happened?'"
Somewhere along the way, the company lost its cool, and Reebok
now faces the task not only of rebuilding its image but of making the
shoes so cool that the kids in the store can't put them down.

Every few months, then, the company's coolhunters go out into 28
the field with prototypes of the upcoming shoes to find out what kids
really like, and come back to recommend the necessary changes. The
prototype of one recent Emmitt Smith shoe, for example, had a piece
of molded rubber on the end of the tongue as a design element; it was
supposed to give the shoe a certain "richness," but the kids said they
thought it looked overbuilt. Then Reebok gave the shoes to the
Boston College football team for wear-testing, and when they got the
shoes back they found out that all the football players had cut out the
rubber component with scissors. As messages go, this was hard to
miss. The tongue piece wasn't cool, and on the final version of the
shoe it was gone. The rule of thumb at Reebok is that if the kids in
Chicago, New York, and Detroit all like a shoe, it's a guaranteed hit.
More than likely, though, the coolhunt is going to turn up subtle differences from city to city, so that once the coolhunters come back the
designers have to find out some way to synthesize what was heard,
and pick out just those things that all the kids seemed to agree on. In
New York, for example, kids in Harlem are more sophisticated and
fashion-forward than kids in the Bronx, who like things a little more
colorful and glitzy. Brooklyn, meanwhile, is conservative and preppy,
more like Washington, D.C. For reasons no one really knows,
Reeboks are coolest in Philadelphia. In Philly, in fact, the Reebok
Classics are so huge they are known simply as National Anthems, as

in "I'll have a pair of blue Anthems in nine and a half." Philadelphia is Reebok's innovator town. From there trends move along the East Coast, trickling all the way to Charlotte, North Carolina.

Reebok has its headquarters in Stoughton, Massachusetts, out- 29 side Boston—in a modern corporate park right off Route 24. There are basketball and tennis courts next to the building, and a health club on the ground floor that you can look directly into from the parking lot. The front lobby is adorned with shrines for all of Reebok's most prominent athletes—shrines complete with dramatic action photographs, their sports jerseys, and a pair of their signature shoes—and the halls are filled with so many young, determinedly athletic people that when I visited Reebok headquarters I suddenly wished I'd packed my gym clothes in case someone challenged me to wind sprints. At Stoughton, I met with a handful of the company's top designers and marketing executives in a long conference room on the third floor. In the course of two hours, they put one pair of shoes after another on the table in front of me, talking excitedly about each sneaker's prospects, because the feeling at Reebok is that things are finally turning around. The basketball shoe that Reebok brought out last winter for Allen Iverson, the star rookie guard for the Philadelphia 76ers, for example, is one of the hottest shoes in the country. Dr. Jay's sold out of Iversons in two days, compared with the week it took the store to sell out of Nike's new Air Jordans. Iverson himself is brash and charismatic and faster from foul line to foul line than anyone else in the league. He's the equivalent of those kids in the East Village who began wearing Hush Puppies way back when. He's an innovator, and the hope at Reebok is that if he gets big enough the whole company can ride back to coolness on his coattails, the way Nike rode to coolness on the coattails of Michael Jordan. That's why Baysie was so excited when the kid said Reebok was try-ing to get butter when he looked at the Rush and the DMX RXT: it was a sign, albeit a small one, that the indefinable, abstract thing called cool was coming back.

When Baysie comes back from a coolhunt, she sits down with 30 marketing experts and sales representatives and designers, and reconnects them to the street, making sure they have the right shoes going to the right places at the right price. When she got back from the Bronx, for example, the first thing she did was tell all these peo-ple they had to get a new men's DMX RXT out, fast, because the kids on the street loved the women's version. "It's hotter than we real-ized," she told them. The coolhunter's job in this instance is very spe-cific. What DeeDee does, on the other hand, is a little more ambitious.

With the L Report, she tries to construct a kind of grand matrix of cool, comprising not just shoes but everything kids like, and not just kids of certain East Coast urban markets but kids all over. DeeDee and her staff put it out four times a year, in six different versions—for New York, Los Angeles, San Francisco, Austin-Dallas, Seattle, and Chicago—and then sell it to manufacturers, retailers, and ad agencies (among others) for twenty thousand dollars a year. They go to each city and find the coolest bars and clubs, and ask the coolest kids to fill out questionnaires. The information is then divided into six categories—You Saw It Here First, Entertainment and Leisure, Clothing and Accessories, Personal and Individual, Aspirations, and Food and Beverages—which are, in turn, broken up into dozens of subcategories, so that Personal and Individual, for example, includes Cool Date, Cool Evening, Free Time, Favorite Possession, and on and on. The information in those subcategories is subdivided again by sex and by age bracket (14–18, 19–24, 25–30), and then, as a control, the L Report gives you the corresponding set of preferences for "mainstream" kids.

Few coolhunters bother to analyze trends with this degree of [31] specificity. DeeDee's biggest competitor, for example, is something called the Hot Sheet, out of Manhattan. It uses a panel of three thousand kids a year from across the country and divides up their answers by sex and age, but it doesn't distinguish between regions, or between trendsetting and mainstream respondents. So what you're really getting is what all kids think is cool—not what cool kids think is cool, which is a considerably different piece of information. Janine Misdom and Joanne DeLuca, who run the Sputnik coolhunting group out of the garment district in Manhattan, meanwhile, favor an entirely impressionistic approach, sending out coolhunters with video cameras to talk to kids on the ground that it's too difficult to get cool kids to fill out questionnaires. Once, when I was visiting the Sputnik girls—as Misdom and DeLuca are known on the street, because they look alike and their first names are so similar and both have the same awesome New York accents—they showed me a video of the girl they believe was the patient zero of the whole eighties revival going on right now. It was back in September of 1993. Joanne and Janine were on Seventh Avenue, outside the Fashion Institute of Technology, doing random street interviews for a major jeans company, and, quite by accident, they ran into this nineteen-year-old raver. She had close-cropped hair, which was green at the top, and at the temples was shaved even closer and dyed pink. She had rings and studs all over her face, and a thick collection of silver tribal jewelry around her neck, and vintage jeans. She looked into the camera and said, "The sixties came in and then the seventies came in and I think it's ready to come back to the eighties. It's totally eighties: the eye makeup, the clothes. It's totally going back to that." Immediately, Joanne and Janine started asking around. "We talked to a few kids on the Lower East Side who said they were feeling the need to start breaking out their old Michael Jackson jackets," Joanne said. "They were joking about it. They weren't doing it yet. But they were going to, you know? They were saying, 'We're getting the urge to break out our Members Only jackets.'" That was right when Joanne and Janine were just starting up; calling the eighties revival was their first big break, and now they put out a full-blown videotaped report twice a year which is a collection of clips of interviews with extremely progressive people.

What DeeDee argues, though, is that cool is too subtle and too 32 variegated to be captured with these kind of broad strokes. Cool is a set of dialects, not a language. The L Report can tell you, for example, that nineteen-to-twenty-four-year-old male trendsetters in Seattle would most like to meet, among others, King Solomon and Dr. Seuss, and that nineteen-to-twenty-four-year-old female trendsetters in San Francisco have turned their backs on Calvin Klein, Nintendo Gameboy, and sex. What's cool right now? Among male New York trendsetters: North Face jackets, rubber and latex, khakis, and the rock band Kiss. Among female trendsetters: ska music, old-lady clothing, and cyber tech. In Chicago, snowboarding is huge among trendsetters of both sexes and all ages. Women over nineteen are into short hair, while those in their teens have embraced mod culture, rock climbing, tag watches, and bootleg pants. In Austin-Dallas, meanwhile, twenty-five-to-thirty-year-old women trendsetters are into hats, heroin, computers, cigars, Adidas, and velvet, while men in their twenties are into video games and hemp. In all, the typical L Report runs over one hundred pages. But with that flood of data comes an obsolescence disclaimer: "The fluctuating nature of the trendsetting market makes keeping up with trends a difficult task." By the spring, in other words, everything may have changed.

The key to coolhunting, then, is to look for cool people first and 33 cool things later, and not the other way around. Since cool things are always changing, you can't look for them, because the very fact they are cool means you have no idea what to look for. What you would be doing is thinking back on what was cool before and extrapolating, which is about as useful as presuming that because the Dow rose ten points yesterday it will rise another ten points today. Cool people, on the other hand, are a constant.

When I was in California, I met Salvador Barbier, who had been 34
described to me by a coolhunter as "the Michael Jordan of skate-
boarding." He was tall and lean and languid, with a cowboy's insou-
ciance, and we drove through the streets of Long Beach at fifteen
miles an hour in a white late-model Ford Mustang, a car he had
bought as a kind of ironic status gesture ("It would look good if I had
a Polo jacket or maybe Nautica," he said) to go with his '62 Econoline
van and his '64 T-bird. Sal told me that he and his friends, who are all
in their mid-twenties, recently took to dressing up as if they were in
eighth grade again and gathering together—having a "rally"—on old
BMX bicycles in front of their local 7-Eleven. "I'd wear muscle shirts,
like Def Leppard or Foghat or some old heavy-metal band, and tight,
tight tapered Levi's, and Vans on my feet—big, like, checkered Vans
or striped Vans or camouflage Vans—and then wristbands and
gloves with the fingers cut off. It was total eighties fashion. You had
to look like that to participate in the rally. We had those denim jackets with patches on the back and combs that hung out the back
pocket. We went without I.D.s, because we'd have to have someone
else buy us beers." At this point, Sal laughed. He was driving really
slowly and staring straight ahead and talking in a low drawl—the
coolhunter's dream. "We'd ride to this bar and I'd have to carry my
bike inside, because we have really expensive bikes, and when we
got inside people would freak out. They'd say, 'Omigod,' and I was
asking them if they wanted to go for a ride on the handlebars. They
were like, 'What is wrong with you. My boyfriend used to dress like
that in the eighth grade!' And I was like, 'He was probably a lot
cooler then, too.'"

This is just the kind of person DeeDee wants. "I'm looking for 35
somebody who is an individual, who has definitely set himself apart
from everybody else, who doesn't look like his peers. I've run into
trendsetters who look completely Joe Regular Guy. I can see Joe
Regular Guy at a club listening to some totally hardcore band playing, and I say to myself 'Omigod, what's that guy doing here?' and
that totally intrigues me, and I have to walk up to him and say, 'Hey,
you're really into this band. What's up?' You know what I mean? I
look at everything. If I see Joe Regular Guy sitting in a coffee shop
and everyone around him has blue hair, I'm going to gravitate
toward him, because, hey, what's Joe Regular Guy doing in a coffee
shop with people with blue hair?"

We were sitting outside the Fred Segal store in West Hollywood. 36
I was wearing a very conservative white Brooks Brothers button-
down and a pair of Levi's, and DeeDee looked first at my shirt and

then my pants and dissolved into laughter: "I mean, I might even go up to you in a cool place."

Picking the right person is harder than it sounds, though. Piney 37 Kahn, who works for DeeDee, says, "There are a lot of people in the gray area. You've got these kids who dress ultra funky and have their own style. Then you realize they're just running after their friends." The trick is not just to be able to tell who is different but to be able to tell when that difference represents something truly cool. It's a gut thing. You have to somehow just know. DeeDee hired Piney because Piney clearly knows: she is twenty-four and used to work with the Beastie Boys and has the formidable self-possession of someone who is not only cool herself but whose parents were cool. "I mean," she says, "they named me after a tree."

Piney and DeeDee said that they once tried to hire someone as a 38 coolhunter who was not, himself, cool, and it was a disaster.

"You can give them the boundaries," Piney explained. "You can 39 say that if people shop at Banana Republic and listen to Alanis Morissette they're probably not trendsetters. But then they might go out and assume that everyone who does that is not a trendsetter, and not look at the other things."

"I mean, I myself might go into Banana Republic and buy a 40 T-shirt," DeeDee chimed in.

Their non-cool coolhunter just didn't have that certain instinct, 41 that sense that told him when it was O.K. to deviate from the manual. Because he wasn't cool, he didn't know cool, and that's the essence of the third rule of cool: you have to be one to know one. That's why Baysie is still on top of this business at forty-one. "It's easier for me to tell you what kid is cool than to tell you what things are cool," she says. But that's all she needs to know. In this sense, the third rule of cool fits perfectly into the second: the second rule says that cool cannot be manufactured, only observed, and the third says that it can only be observed by those who are themselves cool. And, of course, the first rule says that it cannot accurately be observed at all, because the act of discovering cool causes cool to take flight, so if you add all three together they describe a closed loop, the hermeneutic circle of coolhunting, a phenomenon whereby not only can the uncool not see cool but cool cannot even be adequately described to them. Baysie says that she can see a coat on one of her friends and think it's not cool but then see the same coat on DeeDee and think that it is cool. It is not possible to be cool, in other words, unless you are—in some larger sense—already cool, and so the phenomenon that the uncool cannot see and cannot have described to them is also something that they cannot ever attain, because if they did it would no longer be cool. Coolhunting represents the ascendancy, in the marketplace, of high school.

Once, I was visiting DeeDee at her house in Laurel Canyon when 42 one of her L Report assistants, Jonas Vail, walked in. He'd just come back from Niketown on Wilshire Boulevard, where he'd bought seven hundred dollars' worth of the latest sneakers to go with the three hundred dollars' worth of skateboard shoes he'd bought earlier in the afternoon. Jonas is tall and expressionless, with a peacoat, dark jeans, and short-cropped black hair. "Jonas is good," DeeDee says. "He works with me on everything. That guy knows more pop culture. You know: What was the name of the store Mrs. Garrett owned on 'The Facts of Life'? He knows all the names of the extras from eighties sitcoms. I can't believe someone like him exists. He's fucking unbelievable. Jonas can spot a cool person a mile away."

Jonas takes the boxes of shoes and starts unpacking them on the 43 couch next to DeeDee. He picks up a pair of the new Nike ACG hiking boots, and says, "All the Japanese in Niketown were really into these." He hands the shoes to DeeDee.

"Of *course* they were!" she says. "The Japanese are all into the 44 tech-looking shit. Look how exaggerated it is, how bulbous." DeeDee has very ambivalent feelings about Nike, because she thinks its marketing has got out of hand. When she was in the New York Niketown with a girlfriend recently, she says, she started getting light-headed and freaked out. "It's cult, cult, cult. It was like, 'Hello, are we all drinking the Kool-Aid here?'" But this shoe she loves. It's Dr. Jay's in the Bronx all over again. DeeDee turns the shoe around and around in the air, tapping the big clear-blue plastic bubble on the side—the visible Air-Sole unit—with one finger. "It's so fucking rad. It looks like a platypus!" In front of me, there is a pair of Nike's new shoes for the basketball player Jason Kidd.

I pick it up. "This looks . . . cool," I venture uncertainly. 45

DeeDee is on the couch, where she's surrounded by shoeboxes 46 and sneakers and white tissue paper, and she looks up reprovingly because, of course, I don't get it. I can't get it. "Beyooond cool, Maalcolm. Beyooond cool."

3

THE ARTS

WHY THE RECORD INDUSTRY IS IN TROUBLE

Jann S. Wenner

Album sales are now down almost twenty percent from two   1
years ago, and the record business is facing the biggest retail slide
since the Great Depression. Yet rather than seek new ways to market,
price and distribute music, the record labels have raised CD prices
and continued their futile efforts to shut down Internet file-sharing
sites, surely the most important innovation in music technology in
the last twenty years. The industry insists on blaming music fans for
its troubles.

Digital technology is not going away. We are growing accus-   2
tomed to getting our music on demand, through our computers, one
song at a time. The labels have played defense instead of embracing
the Internet age and have spent millions of dollars trying to shut
down trading sites—from Napster to Kazaa—rather than recognize
the potential of the Web to market, promote and sell music. They've
done the same thing with Internet radio, lobbying for prohibitive
royalty rates that threaten to push thousands of independent stations—potentially great places to promote new and niche artists—
out of business.

Several labels, including Sony and Universal, are offering limited   3
songs online for ninety-nine cents each. But this is not enough: The
labels must get together to put all of their music online—from the
newest singles to the oldest catalog material—and allow fans to
download what they want, for a fair price. "The kids have already
stated. 'All of the music, all of the time,'" says Lyor Cohen, president
of Island Def Jam Music Group. "Meanwhile, the record companies
have responded with, 'Some of the music, some of the time.'"

A new distribution system could work like basic cable television, 4 where users download as much as they want monthly, with premium offers and pay-per-download-style events. If 10 million people sign up for the new service, gross revenues could be enormous, with little of the current costs that record companies incur for manufacturing, marketing and retailing.

Still, the labels' unwillingness to move online, and their insis- 5 tence on keeping prices too high, are just the obvious parts of the problem. The more complicated matter is the quality of the music itself. Labels have been unable to find ways to develop and broadly expose new bands and are too willing to put out albums with only two or three good songs. How many people spend eighteen dollars for a CD, then discover that the one song getting played on the radio or MTV is the single decent track? That has to happen only a few times before fans start looking for more cost-efficient ways to get music.

The labels say they can't compete with free—that CD-burning 6 piracy and file swapping are the principal reasons for the industry's troubles. They claim that CD burning alone has cost $4.3 billion in lost revenues, and that file swapping costs them billions more. But there are no conclusive studies to prove that digital downloading cuts into album sales—in fact, some studies suggest that free downloading encourages fans to hear and buy more music. Further, there is ample evidence that the most active music fans today are both the biggest downloaders and the biggest music buyers. So why is the record industry going to war against its best customers?

While the costs of CD manufacturing has dropped—it costs 7 record labels about forty cents to manufacture a CD, packaging included—retail prices have continued to rise. And consumers aren't willing to spend twenty dollars for a CD with two or three decent tracks. It's a question of simple marketplace common sense: Labels must give consumers product they want at a fair price. And artists play a role in this, too. Successful musicians have the power to demand and participate in price reductions for their releases, past and present.

The music business should take a cue from the hugely profitable 8 DVD industry. In the past year, prices for DVDs have dropped, from about twenty dollars to seventeen dollars—and many DVDs come with excellent bonus materials that give additional value for the money.

Some of the year's biggest new artists, such as Ashanti and 9 Norah Jones, have benefited from lower prices: $8.99 to $13.99. Avril

Lavigne's debut, *Let Go*, sold for $5.99 in some outlets. All three of these artists are currently among the Top Twenty in the *Billboard* 200, and their success shows that people are still willing to pay for music. But they're not willing to be ripped off.

If the labels continue to blame the public for their own mistakes,   10 rather than lowering prices and finding ways to effectively deliver music online, then music fans will grow even more alienated than they already are. And then, by comparison, the current sales slump will look like a boom.

Cop Out? The Media, "Cop Killer," and the Deracialization of Black Rage (Constructing [Mis]Representations)

Christopher Sieving

For about seven weeks in the sizzling summer of 1992, the most 1
contentious issue in American society was not about who deserved
to be elected to the presidency in the upcoming election or what
should be done to rebuild the nation's second largest city after it had
suffered the worst civil disturbances in the United States in a century
and a half. Instead, the most hotly debated concern involved a black,
thirtyish rap artist named Tracy Marrow (better known as Ice-T) and
the multimedia conglomerate (Time Warner) that represented him.
Specifically, at issue was a song Ice-T recorded for Sire/Warner Bros.
Records with his thrash-metal band, Body Count. The sentiments
evoked in the lyrics to "Cop Killer," Ice-T's detractors cried, consti-
tuted an exhortation to kill police officers. For two months, the
recording industry, public officials, police groups, and civil liberties
advocates squared off over the right to express and circulate these
ideas in public, culminating with Ice-T's "voluntary" withdrawal of
the song on July 28.

The public debate over "Cop Killer" was unique in many 2
respects, but perhaps one of its most striking characteristics was that
only a tiny minority of Americans actually heard the song at all. "Cop
Killer" was not played on the radio, it was not shown on MTV, and
the album on which it appeared (*Body Count*) sold fewer than 500,000
copies before the song was permanently withdrawn from distribution. For this reason, the key issues for a cultural analysis of the "Cop
Killer" controversy involve how the song was put into discourse and
circulated in other forms of media. If "Cop Killer" was too "hot" for
direct experience, the American press was more than willing to supply its own mediated versions. This is how L.A. County Supervisor
Gloria Molina, one of the many elected officials who called on Time
Warner to have "Cop Killer" withdrawn, initially encountered it: "I
have not listened to this song, but I am convinced by what I've read
in news accounts that this is a totally inappropriate rap (sic) song"
(Goldberg 1992, M2).

The willingness with which interested parties accepted versions 3
of Ice-T's words at least once removed from the context he had
intended them to appear in should remind one of Foucault's ideas on
the social dimensions of discourse, as modified by John Fiske. In an
age marked by a promiscuity of image and sound representations, no
person may dictate the ways in which they are represented. "The
way that experience, and the events that constitute it, is put into discourse," Fiske (1996, 4) writes, "is never determined by the nature of
experience itself, but always by the social power to give it one set of
meanings rather than another." Ice-T's experience, his black knowledge (to use another of Foucault's terms) of the policing system in
Los Angeles, entered into dramatic contestation with white power. To
retain its status of truth, white power had to repress Ice-T's black
knowledge by seizing control of it and making it mean in very different ways. To a large extent, it succeeded.

The explosive racial dimensions of the "Cop Killer" affair also 4
dictate a close examination of the media's part in fanning the flames
of controversy. The ways in which candidates Dan Quayle, Bill
Clinton, and George Bush employed the press to attack "Cop Killer,"
Ice-T, and black culture in general have been duly noted and are con-
sonant with the methods by which the presidential and vice presidential candidates used race as a wedge issue in 1992. Furthermore,
some critics, including Robin D.G. Kelley (1996, 131), have also noted
the media's substantive role in creating and putting into discourse
the notion of a black, criminalized "underclass," that shadowy, neb-
ulous body responsible for all of America's social ills.

While accusations of the white-controlled American media's 5
complicity in the promulgation of '90s-style institutional racism are
well founded, it is also true, as Tricia Rose (1994, 101) alludes to in her
study of rap and black culture, *Black Noise*, that the current-day system of mass cultural production—"mass-mediated and mass-distrib-
uted"—grants oppressed groups far greater access to popular media
than previously possible. "The media" are not a homogeneous blob,
devouring all potential discourses that run counter to the ideology of
capitalist enterprise. Rather, they are a site of struggle, analogous to
Gramsci's notion of "common sense," as explained by Stuart Hall
(1980, 20–21). The conservative Right's "family values" battled Ice-
T's black consciousness in the media for a place within the common
sense of the American public. The fact that Ice-T's black consciousness lost the battle—his words erased from the public record—does

not mean that the war is unwinnable. Through a close analysis of the strategies and countertactics used by both sides in the "Cop Killer" dispute, I hope to clarify how Ice-T's case was weakened by the misguided attempts of his defenders to deracialize "Cop Killer." Their disarticulation of lower-class black struggle from the debate mirrored, and thus empowered, the strategies employed by their detractors. In analyzing how this was accomplished, I hope to provide suggestions on how to avoid similar tactical mistakes in the racial and cultural clashes of the future.

Body Count was released by Sire/Warner Bros. in March 1992. 6 The first album recorded by Ice-T's rock band, it was his first group project for the label after four gold-selling solo albums. The album's tracks, all recorded between September and December 1991, were mostly versions of songs the group had performed on tour with the previous summer's Lollapalooza festival. Body Count closed with "Cop Killer," a staple of the band's live show. In a spoken-word lead-in, Ice-T "dedicated" this final track to "every cop that has ever taken advantage of somebody, beat 'em down or hurt 'em" out of blind prejudice or race hatred (Body Count 1992b). Ice-T's lyrics (the music was written by lead guitarist Ernie C.), printed in full in the accompanying CD booklet, forcefully dramatized the vengeful intent of the song's narrator. Switching between first- and second-person address, the would-be Cop Killer describes the ritual of preparing for an ambush ("I got my black gloves on / I got my ski mask on") before serving notice to his target: "I know your family's grieving, but tonight we get even." The narrator's motivation for settling the score is, at first, purely personal ("A pig stopped me for nuthin'!"); later, a call-and-response chorus suggests a larger, more broadly social revenge: "Fuck the police, for Rodney King / Fuck the police, for my dead homies" (Body Count 1992a).

Such sentiments raised few eyebrows prior to the late spring of 7 1992—the period of L.A.'s black and Latino uprisings in the wake of the acquittals in the Rodney King trial. In early June, however, "Cop Killer" was condemned publicly for the first time: a Dallas police captain, writing in his column for the Dallas Police Association newsletter, urged his readers to "boycott any and all Time Warner products and movies until such time as they have recalled this tape" (Duffy and Orr 1992). This suggestion was immediately taken up and amplified by the Combined Law Enforcement Association of Texas (CLEAT). CLEAT's press conference on June 11 at Six Flags amusement park in Arlington broke the story nationwide. In calling for a boycott of Time Warner entertainment (including Six Flags), CLEAT director Mark Clark specified who his organization was targeting (and previewed a major discursive strategy of the anti-"Cop Killer" forces): "Our quarrel is not with Ice-T, but with the beautiful people that run Time Warner who like to present themselves as being in the business of family entertainment . . . the people who made a decision to reap huge dividends by distributing music that advocates the murder of police officers" (Philips 1992a). Within a week, the New York State Sheriff's Association joined ranks with CLEAT, and Alabama Governor Guy Hunt called for a statewide ban on selling the *Body Count* album. This initial burst of protest culminated with Dan Quayle's attack on Time Warner for "making money off a record that is suggesting it's O.K. to kill cops" at a luncheon for the National Association of Radio Talk Show Hosts ("Vice President Calls Corporation Wrong" 1992).

Why "Cop Killer"? Why did this song prove to be such an attrac- 8 tive target for conservative forces? Why did the formation of a strong counterdiscourse in opposition to Ice-T's ideas come to be seen by the nation's power brokers as a top national priority? The motives were many and varied. The justification most often given for opposing the distribution of "Cop Killer"—the fear that it would incite murder and mayhem—was undoubtedly a genuine one for some. But their concern does not explain why this particular work—one of countless mediated representations of violence—was singled out for special criticism.

Three major contextual factors brought about the targeting of 9 "Cop Killer" at this time. One was the growing white hostility toward certain types of rap music. The increasingly confrontational style of several major rap artists put the genre on a collision course with white authorities by the late 1980s. The outcry over Professor Griff's (of Public Enemy) anti-Semitic remarks in a *Washington Times* interview, the NWA song "—tha Police" (which Ice-T cites in "Cop Killer"), and the 2 Live Crew album *As Nasty as They Wanna Be* influenced the increasingly negative coverage of rap in the mainstream press. As public hysteria broke out over the nation's perceived inability to contain its hyperviolent black population, rap music came to be seen as the original sin of the underclass. The equation of black crime with black culture was made explicit by pundits such as George Will (1990), who implied that the sexual violence depicted in 2 Live Crew's lyrics influenced the infamous Central Park "wilding" incident of April 1989. And Timothy White (1991), in a controversial *Billboard* editorial, condemned Ice Cube's 1991 album *Death Certificate* for advocating violence against Koreans and Jews. Although *Body*

Count was not a rap group (and "Cop Killer" was not a rap song), it was drawn into this nexus by virtue of employing Ice-T (noted "gangsta" rapper, who had previously been singled out by Parents' Music Resource Center head Tipper Gore for the "vileness of his message") (Donnelly 1992, 66) as its lead singer.

The L.A. rebellion of late April and early May 1992 further [10] helped to foreground in the minds of white Americans the link between rap artists and black insurrection. In the absence of "rational" (white) explanations for the destruction of South Central L.A., television, radio, and print coverage of the rebellion relied heavily on the contextualizing commentary of rappers, those whose music provided, in Alan Light's (1992a, 15) words, the only "source . . . available to communicate the attitudes of inner-city America to the white mainstream." Ice-T quickly emerged as one of the "hard-edged rappers" the *Washington Post* later designated as "[spokespersons] for the black lower class, delegates of America's angry youth" (Mills 1992, B1). Yet, for all the likeminded opinions expressed in the media on the premonitory power of L.A. hard-core, an equal number of dissenters felt that rap had incited, as opposed to predicted, the violence that followed the first Rodney King verdict. Ice Cube's (1991) rap "Black Korea," an attack on South Central's Korean store owners, was frequently cited by columnists for its couplet "Pay respect to the Black fist / Or we'll burn your store right down to a crisp." For some white Americans, residual hostility toward the rioters and "looters" surely fed the hostility toward those black cultural voices who claimed to represent them.

Finally, Bill Clinton's criticisms of rapper / activist Sister Souljah [11] (Lisa Williamson), occurring just three days prior to Quayle's attack on "Cop Killer," helped to legitimate the vilification of rappers as an election year discursive strategy. Democratic candidate Clinton, following Jesse Jackson at a Rainbow Coalition convention, denounced remarks made by Souljah in a *Washington Post* interview ("I mean, if black people kill black people every day, why not have a week and kill white people?") (Mills 1992, B1). While it may have been the case (as was widely believed) that Clinton was more concerned about his appeal with conservative voters than about the impact of Souljah's words, the immediate result of his Rainbow Coalition address was to put rap on the political map. In the scramble for swing issues (à la Willie Horton) they could claim as their own, Republicans were only too receptive to the increasingly vocal cries of the upholders of law and order.

In the wake of Dan Quayle's condemnation on June 19, police   12
oganizations across the country pledged to support CLEAT's call for
a Time Warner boycott; in addition, the 23,000-member National
Sheriffs Association spearheaded a movement to persuade sympa-
thetic law enforcement organizations with Time Warner investments
to divest ("Quayle, Congressmen" 1992, 83). State officials began calling on Time Warner to withdraw *Body Count* from the marketplace.
In Los Angeles, councilwoman (and congressional candidate) Joan
Milke Flores and the Los Angeles Police Protective League—echoed
later by the Los Angeles Police Commission—motioned for just such
a ban in a city council meeting (Philips 1992b). A Florida sheriff peti-
tioned the state attorney general to investigate whether Time
Warner's marketing of "Cop Killer" violated sedition laws, an action
also advocated by Iran-Contra figure Oliver North ("Count Rises"
1992, 74). Perhaps most significantly (and ominously), sixty congressional representatives (including three Democrats and fifty-seven
Republicans) sent a letter to Time Warner vice president Jeanette
Lerman stating that the conglomerate's "decision to disseminate
these despicable lyrics advocating the murder of police officers is
unconscionable" ("Quayle, Congressmen" 1992, 83).

As the controversy was reaching fever pitch, Time Warner held   13
its annual shareholders' meeting on July 16 at the Regent Beverly
Wilshire Hotel in Beverly Hills. As had been anticipated for weeks,
the meeting was infiltrated by angry police group representatives
and conservative spokespersons such as 2 Live Crew prosecuting
attorney Jack Thompson (who was roundly booed) and Charlton
Heston, who recited the lyrics to "Cop Killer" and "KKK Bitch" (a
second *Body Count* song) to the stunned stockholders. Time Warner
president and co-CEO Gerald Levin fielded hostile inquiries indoors,
while outside the hotel around thirty protesters (some of whom
reportedly chanted "Ice-T should be put to death") (Trent 1992) pick-
eted the corporation (Morris 1992b, 71).

The result of this highly visible, direct confrontation was perhaps   14
surprising, at least for the protesters: Time Warner refused to budge.
In public, Levin continued to uphold the right of his artist to express
himself in accordance with his First Amendment rights. In response,
his opposition turned up the heat even further. Following a July 21
appearance by Ice-T on *The Arsenio Hall Show*, Hall's office received
a flood of threatening phone calls from angry viewers (Shaw 1992).
On July 23, *The Today Show* fanned the flames of the controversy by
broadcasting excerpts from a home video of Ice-T addressing a

crowd of L.A. urban dwellers on the third day of the Los Angeles rebellion; in the video, Ice-T tells the crowd that "police ain't shit to me and never will be. . . . They're a Gestapo organization in Los Angeles and until you start taking them cops down out here in the street, then y'all still fucking pissing in the wind, you know what I'm sayin'?" (Morris 1992c, 83). Most seriously, as reported in *Entertainment Weekly*, Time Warner's headquarters had received at least one bomb threat, while "one exec received a phone death threat from an anonymous bigot who called him a 'nigger-loving Jew'" (Sandow 1992).

As he would later recount in his book *The Ice Opinion*, the various 15 threats made to Time Warner executives and to his own fifteen-year-old daughter played a pivotal part in Ice-T's decision to voluntarily pull "Cop Killer" from the *Body Count* album (Ice-T and Siegmund 1994, 176). In his press conference of July 28, Ice-T announced that Time Warner would cease the distribution of *Body Count* in its original form. Subsequent editions of the album would not contain the "Cop Killer" track.

Jon Pareles (1992b, C13), writing in *The New York Times* the day 16 following Ice-T's press conference, was one of many who appreciated the irony of the "Cop Killer" protest, acknowledging the protesters' "part in building the album's popularity." The notoriety bestowed on the *Body Count* album clearly boosted its sales; in the month prior to Ice-T's announcement, *Body Count* had sold about 100,000 copies, despite the fact that at least a half-dozen major music retailers refused to carry it. (Barry Layne [1992], writing one month earlier in *The Hollywood Reporter*, dryly noted that "the first fruits of [CLEAT's] action . . . was a tripling of '*Body Count*' album sales in the Lone Star state.") The demand for the album immediately intensified upon news of its withdrawal; by the beginning of August, *Body Count* surged from number seventy-three to number twenty-six on *Billboard*'s pop album chart, and runs on the original version were reported in several cities ("A Run on Ice-T's Album" 1992).

So what did these police organizations and public officials gain 17 from publicizing an album and a song that might otherwise have barely registered on the cultural imaginary? Quite a bit, in fact, and a close reading of the discursive strategies these white-dominated groups employed during the "Cop Killer" controversy throws some of these suppressed motivations into sharp relief.

"Cop Killer" posed a problem for those who wished to demonize 18 it. It was written and performed by a black group; thus, those who called for its censoring risked appearing overtly racist. The musician who wrote the lyrics was primarily associated with rap music, a form increasingly unpopular with "middle" America; however, the song was not, strictly speaking, a rap song. Furthermore, the sentiments of "Cop Killer" were protected by the First Amendment, and the song had the backing of a gigantic, American-owned conglomerate—a powerful symbol of free market enterprise.

How, then, could "Cop Killer" be fought? What strategies could be employed, and what sentiments could be exploited? Not surprisingly, the strategies the Right eventually settled on were, for the most part, profoundly deracializing. Even though racial difference had played an undeniable role in the creation, transmission, and reception (an *Entertainment Weekly* poll found that "nearly 60 percent of nonblacks said they were angry at [Ice-T], as opposed to 34 percent of blacks") (Sandow 1992) of "Cop Killer," its critics had to recode that difference as something "beyond" race. The discursive strategy summed up by the now-familiar tenet "race had nothing to do with it" that had been deployed, with some success, just weeks earlier in the official white reaction to the L.A. rebellion. *The Source* editor James Bernard (1992) noted how the news media's riot coverage had focused almost exclusively on the "mindless" destruction of black-owned businesses as "a particularly tragic example of Black-on-Black violence, that these people wouldn't even give their own hardworking middle class a chance" (p. 41). In doing so, reporters and newscasters implied (and, at times, explicitly stated) that the rebellion was not motivated by anger over racial injustice but by sheer lawlessness, or that it was, as *Billboard*'s Chris Morris (1992a) described it, simply "beyond rational explanation." It is no surprise, then, that this discourse of deracialization was applied in the attacks on Ice-T's black rage. What is surprising is how often the defenses against these attacks were equally deracializing.

Reaccentualization

As the U.S. market economy and its institutions have become more integrated over the past several decades, the importance of language as a way to construct one's identity, to create one's own space— in sum, to serve as a tactic of resistance—has exploded. Perhaps the most helpful theoretical explication of the defiant social uses of language is found in Russian philosopher Volosinov's (1973) *Marxism and the Philosophy of Language*—particularly in his conception of accentuality. He argues that words do not have predetermined, fixed meanings; rather, the "meaning of a word is determined entirely by its context. . . . It is precisely a word's multiaccentuality that makes it a living thing" (pp. 79, 81). Volosinov's observation that "in the alternating lines of a dialogue, the same word may figure in two mutually clashing contexts" is certainly applicable to the debate over the meaning of the "Cop Killer"'s lyrics (p. 80). These words, spoken with a black accent by Ice-T, are spoken with a white accent by Charlton Heston and thus "mean" in vastly different ways. Heston's July 16 reaccenting of "Cop Killer" verifies Volosinov's idea that accent is where the social politics of the speaker enter the linguistic system. Heston's imposition of the voice of white authority so completely changed the original black meaning of the song that, for many of the shareholders in attendance, the song now seemed to contain its own rebuttal. An L.A. resident who heard Heston's recitation over KFI radio certified the objectives of this reaccenting in her letter to *Los Angeles Times* "It was rather startling to listen to such words coming from the magnificent voice of Moses, Andrew Jackson, John the Baptist, but I am grateful to him for expressing this aspect of the album" (Agreda 1992).

As a counterstrategy, Heston's reaccenting method is much subtler than the explicit race baiting found in a contemporaneous piece for the *National Review*, in which James Bowman (1992, 37) doubts "that Sister Souljah or Ice-T or even the Los Angeles ghetto dwellers for whom both of them have at various times purported to speak are actually oppressed; rather, they have inherited from their ancestors, who were, a form of speech and imagery characterized by a kind of fantastical moral chiaroscuro." In the end, Heston's is clearly the more effective strategy, as it was readily taken up by the mainstream; the attempt to account for racially differentiated modes of reception is relegated to the pages of a marginal right-wing periodical. 21

It seems apparent, then, that one way to counter the widespread deracialization of "Cop Killer" would have been to call attention to its black accent and to the ways in which meaning is struggled over by blacks and whites. Thomas Kochman's (1981) account of "fighting words" in his influential book *Black and White Styles in Conflict* illustrates the cultural framework that governs the codes used in urban black language. Kochman's research on the use of fighting words in both black and white communities demonstrates that 22

> angry verbal disputes [or woofing], even those involving insults and threats, can be maintained by blacks at the verbal level without violence necessarily resulting. . . . On the streets [woofing's]

purpose is to gain, without actually having to become violent, the respect and fear from others that is often won through physical combat. (pp. 48, 49)

Ice-T himself says as much when he declares that "within my community, rap is verbal combat. We get around a lot of fights and aggression simply by talking" (Ice-T and Siegmund 1994, 103).

The failure of Ice-T's defenders to use a theoretical framework [23] such as Kochman's to explain the verbal arrows slung throughout *Body Count* is perhaps attributable to the white community's inability to conceive of fighting words as anything but an invitation to physical aggression; according to Kochman (1981, 48), "whites tend to see the public expression of hostility as a point on a words-action continuum." The furor over "Cop Killer" illustrates the full extent of white ignorance, conscious or not, of what John Fiske (1996, 187) terms "sociocultural conventions that are clear to [their] native speakers." During the controversy, Ice-T repeatedly asserted that language is raced and expressed his frustration with having to explain his lyrics to whites. Before deciding to withdraw the *Body Count* album, Ice-T told *Time* that "[white America] shouldn't sweat us on what words we use with each other. I hate to say rap is a black thing, but sometimes it is" (Donnelly 1992, 66). Unfortunately, white America refused to listen to his admonitions.

Decontextualization

The reaccenting of "Cop Killer" by white voices was mirrored by [24] the selective excerpting of the song's lyrics by its opponents. By extracting certain lines (or "sound bites," to borrow a phrase) from the context of the song, the album, and Ice-T's body of work in their entirety, Ice-T's opponents more easily succeeded in making his statements fit their own discursive project, one that explained the song in terms of brutal lawlessness. Bill Clinton put the strategy of decontextualization to use in his attack on Sister Souljah; not only did Clinton ignore the meaning of Souljah's *Washington Post* comments within the larger context of the L.A. rebellion, but he ignored the whole of the quotation itself:

I mean, if black people kill black people every day, why not have a week and kill white people? You understand what I'm saying? In other words, white people, this government and that mayor were well aware of the fact that black people were dying every day in

Los Angeles under gang violence. So if you're a gang member and you would normally be killing somebody, why not kill a white person? Do you think that somebody thinks that white people are better, or above dying, when they would kill their own kind? (Mills 1992, B1)

The Today Show aided Clinton's efforts by broadcasting only one 25 segment of Sister Souljah's music video, a segment in which a white police officer is shot and killed by a black woman (Leo 1992). The context for the character's action—the reimplementation of slavery in the United States—was excised from NBC's "sampling."

To my knowledge, the lyrics to "Cop Killer" were never 26 reprinted in full in any mainstream or "general-interest" American magazine or newspaper (even though they were readily available to anyone who took a look at the album's sleeve). *The Los Angeles Times'* initial report on the boycott excerpted what would become perhaps the most reprinted verse of the song, "I got my 12 gauge sawed off / I got my headlights turned off / I'm 'bout to bust some shots off / I'm 'bout to dust some cops off" (Philips 1992a). Paul M. Walters (1992) repeated this excerpt in his *Times* op-ed piece of July 8, adding that "the verse and chorus that follow are far too vulgar to discuss." This sentiment was apparently shared by Mike Royko (1995, 175), who deleted the "obscenities" from the portion of the song he cited in his June 23 syndicated column, and by the National Rifle Association, whose full-page advertisements in the June 26 *USA Today* and the June 28 *Washington Times* quoted the chorus to "Cop Killer" as "DIE PIG DIE! (expletive) the Police . . . don't be a (expletive). Have some (expletive) courage . . . I'm a (expletive) Cop Killer!" ("White Time Warner Counts Its Money" 1992).

The forced dislocation of the Cop Killer's murderous intentions 27 from the rest of his narrative served to frame his imagined crimes as groundless. The intent of extracting, for example, only the words "'bout to dust some cops off" and "die, pigs (sic), die" from the song, as was the case in an Associated Press report of June 19, was to justify the application of just such a meaning ("Rapper Ice-T Defends Song" 1992). Thus, Michael Kinsley (1992), writing in both the *New Republic* ("Momma Dearest" 1992) and *Time,* can point to the call-and-response chorus and the line "I know your family's grievin'—f—'em" as evidence that "Cop Killer"'s message is that "premeditated acts of revenge against random cops . . . is a justified response to police brutality" (Kinsley 1992). Few media pundits agreed with Ice-T's claim ("better you than me . . . if it's gonna be me, then better you") (Ice-T and Siegmund 1994, 168) that the song's protagonist acts in self-defense; none, to my knowledge, excerpted the spoken-word track that prefaced the song on the *Body Count* CD.

Like the Rodney King and the Latasha Harlins videos, with which there are intriguing parallels, "Cop Killer" was almost never publicly "aired" in its entirety; the public knew little, even during the height of the furor, of what preceded the "fuck the police" chorus. Few of Ice-T's defenders, in fact, looked to the larger context of the album (the only way in which "Cop Killer" could be experienced, as it received no radio play and was not commercially available as a single); had they done so, they would have discovered a song titled "The Winner Loses," which puts forth an unequivocally anti-drug statement at odds with white America's conception of the narcoticized young black male. While it should be apparent why the anti-"Cop Killer" contingent felt it necessary to suppress Ice-T's larger critique of racially differentiated policing, it is less understandable why Ice-T's defenders failed to reintroduce this critique into the context of the debate. 28

Articulation with Sexism and Racism

Volosinov's (1973) shifting of the social struggle paradigm from the traditional Marxists' class-versus-class model to a more heterogeneous subordinated model allows for the cultural analyst to admit that a step forward in racial politics may represent a step backward in gender politics. John Fiske's (1996, 66) notion of multiaxiality, informed by the realization that "because power is everywhere, it flows along all the axes of social difference," modifies Volosinov's and Foucault's ideas through observing that the knowledge flowing along a single axis of power often works by repressing other knowledge. Critics such as Robin D. G. Kelley (1996, 143) understand this when they qualify their endorsements of contemporary urban black culture, such as rap, with stinging critiques of the misogyny and homophobia of several leading black artists (including Ice-T). It is clear even to rap's defenders that rap's struggle over race cannot be won by repressing the gender struggle, as many male rappers have discovered. 29

Although "Cop Killer" makes no mention of gender issues, critics frequently articulated its message with the misogyny (alleged or otherwise) found elsewhere on *Body Count*, in Ice-T's rap music, and in mass culture in general. The editors of the *Los Angeles Times* placed 30

"Cop Killer . . . in the dubious tradition of a long line of exploitative commercial work, along with heavy-metal songs that bash gays, women or minorities" ("Outrage and Ice-T" 1992); Sheila James Kuehl (1992) added that "like too much of rap, the cuts before and after 'Cop Killer' are an insistent demand, a veritable how-to, of mutilated women." Kuehl, a director at the California Women's Law Center, enriches the debate by bringing the question of woman-bashing to the table, but her more hyperbolic statements are not far removed from the outright distortions advanced by Charlton Heston (1992), who falsely asserted that "KKK Bitch" advocated the raping of women and the sodomizing of "little girls."

More problematic than accusations of sexism, however, is the 31 articulation of black rap with racism against whites. David Samuels's (1991, 28) assertion (voiced in a notorious 1991 *New Republic* cover story on "the black music that isn't either") that rap reduces racism to "fashion" is typical of the rhetoric that asserts that contemporary racism is the product of inflammatory black people, with whites serving as the victims. "Cop Killer" was frequently articulated (and, by implication, equated) with anti-Semitic expression, despite the fact that several Time Warner executives—those who most consistently defended Ice-T's work—were Jewish. At the July 16 Time Warner shareholders meeting, Charlton Heston asked Gerald Levin, a Jew, "[if] that line were 'Die, die, die, Kike, die,' would Time Warner defend it then?" while CLEAT president Ron DeLord compared Time Warner executives to Joseph Goebbels (Morris 1992b, 71).

Another favorite strategy of critics of Ice-T and Sister Souljah— 32 including Bill Clinton (Philips 1992c, Calendar 6), John Leo (1992), and Barbara Ehrenreich (1992)—was to link their black adversaries with ex-Klansman and defeated Louisiana gubernatorial candidate David Duke. *The New Republic* even linked "Cop Killer" to George Bush's infamous Willie Horton ad ("Momma Dearest" 1992). These types of strategies served to disarticulate white, illegal policing methods from public discussions of racism. The qualitative difference between the racist effects of, on one hand, lynchings and the Holocaust and, on the other hand, black resistance to racially motivated police brutality in Los Angeles was never explained.

Corporatization

Perhaps the most common deracializing strategy used by Ice-T's 33 opponents during the "Cop Killer" controversy was one of corporatization, or the transference of blame for "Cop Killer"'s potential ill effects from its author to the company that distributed it. The idea that the kinds of messages black rap acts choose to advance are dictated by their white employers is one that had gained significant credibility within the white media by the summer of 1992; David Samuels's (1991) *New Republic* article had perhaps the most success in popularizing this theory.

A strategy such as this might seem counter to the conservative agenda. However, if one adopts Gramscian notions of "hegemony" and "common sense," it becomes easier to understand how conservative capitalists could recast the issue as a referendum on corporate ethics. Stuart Hall (1980, 16) has remarked on how Gramsci's conceptualization of hegemony "implies that the actual social or political force which becomes decisive in a moment of organic crisis . . . will have a complex social composition. . . . Its basis of unity will have to be, not an automatic one, given by its position in the mode of economic production, but rather a 'system of alliances.'" Under late capitalism, there may be (and frequently are) splits within social groups lumped together by ideology theorists under the category of "ruling class"; the alliance between corporate America and the political Right forged along the economic axis is susceptible to breakdown along the cultural, moral, or legal axes. 34

The "Cop Killer" case is perhaps the clearest manifestation of this principle from this decade. In Foucauldian terms, Ice-T's black knowledge entered into contestation with white knowledge; to retain its status as "troth," white knowledge found it necessary to repress that of Ice-T. However, in order for white power to operate at maximum efficacy within a hegemonic order, it has to exercise its power "invisibly." The problem, then, for these white interests lay in the fact that the censoring of an artwork, especially one created by blacks, is bound to be very visible. By recoding the debate as an issue of ethics, Quayle, Heston, and their compatriots were allowed to talk about race through nonracial discourse. 35

From the very beginning, those opposed to "Cop Killer" couched their opposition in terms of corporate responsibility. When Ice-T addressed his audience at the New Music Seminar in New York on June 19 and stated "if the cops got a problem, let them come after me, not Time Warner," Mark Clark of CLEAT responded in *The New York Times* that the issue "is Time Warner making a corporate decision to make a profit off of a song that advocates the murder of police officers and they are the ones we are going to attempt to hold accountable" (Rule 1992, C16). In his speech of the same day, Dan Quayle 36 implied that the inability of the U.S. government to revoke Ice-T's free speech rights dictates that Ice-T's sponsor be targeted in his stead ("Vice President Calls Corporation Wrong" 1992). As was the case in his Murphy Brown speech one month earlier (a speech primarily comprising his observations on the causes of the L.A. rebellion), Quayle avoided charges of election year race baiting by recoding race problems into the effects of the nation's poverty of values. George Bush echoed Quayle's strategy two weeks later at an appearance at a new Drug Enforcement Administration office in Manhattan. "I stand against those who use films or records or television or video games to glorify killing law enforcement officers," Bush proclaimed. "It is wrong for any company—I don't care how noble the name of the company—it is wrong for any company to issue records that approve of killing law enforcement officers" (Rosenthal 1992). The will with which police organizations avoided assigning responsibility to Ice-T reached its height after the artist decided to pull the song, when a representative of the Los Angeles Police Protective League lauded Ice-T for showing "more intestinal fortitude than Time Warner" (Cusolito 1992).

Stuart Hall (1986, 53) conceives of articulation as the formation of [37] linkages, "the form of the connection that can make a unity of two different elements, under certain conditions." The fluid status of any one articulation necessitates the articulation of elements that, in that particular combination, expose the artificiality of the dominant articulation. In recoding "Cop Killer" as the product of an unethical corporation, Quayle and his colleagues disarticulated what Ice-T's defenders needed, but barely attempted, to rearticulate: the links between black hostility toward police officers and the racist system of policing in the United States.

This is not to say that all of those who opposed the distribution [38] of "Cop Killer" employed the strategies of deracialization to denigrate it before the eyes of middle America. Some critics, such as James Bowman (1992) in the *National Review*, risked accusations of racism by drawing articulations between the (presumed) black audience for *Body Count* and the white stereotype of the hyperviolent, narcoticized black criminal. Doug Elder, president of a Houston police organization, warned that "Cop Killer," when mixed "with the summer, the violence and a little drugs (sic) . . . [will] unleash a reign of terror on communities all across this country," while the head of the Fraternal Order of Police opined that "people who ride around all night and use crack cocaine and listen to rap music that talks about killing cops—it's bound to pump them up" (Donnelly 1992, 66;

Philips 1992b). These articulations are relatively oblique compared with Rush Limbaugh's: On his syndicated radio show, Limbaugh labeled Ice-T's fans "savages and the people who beat up Reginald Denny" (Pollack 1992).

A more subtle form of racialization was performed by the count- 39 less number of reporters, officials, and spokespersons who referred to "Cop Killer" and *Body Count* as rap music rather than metal. Rose's (1994, 130) claim that, within white discourse, metal fans are "victims of its influence" whereas rap fans "victimize us" helps to clarify the purpose behind the shift in labeling. Ice-T is thus correct to assert that the word rap was used during the "Cop Killer" debate to "[conjure] up scary images of Black Ghetto" (Ice-T and Siegmund 1994, 170); even the widespread, less misleading use of the designation "rapper Ice-T" served a similar end.

And yet the tracks on *Body Count* are rap, in a certain sense; more 40 specifically, *Body Count* is a "rock album with a rap mentality," as Ice-T himself has suggested (Light 1992b, 30). Sans sampling, the rap "mentality" manifests itself on *Body Count* not only in the gritty, urban scenarios carried over from Ice-T's solo projects but in Ice's clipped, decidedly nonmelodic vocal delivery. I wish to suggest that the considerable fuss raised by Ice-T and his comrades over the media's use of the term rap to categorize "Cop Killer" is misdirected and in fact serves to obscure the debate's more significant implications as explained throughout this article.

The fact that Ice-T's defenders repeatedly, if unknowingly, par- 41 ticipated in obscuring these implications is perhaps the most revealing aspect of the media coverage of the controversy. A range of tactics was used to discredit the conservative attacks on "Cop Killer," yet for the most part these avoided assessing the efficacy of Ice-T's message as a strategy of resistance. Instead, many in the pro-Ice-T faction chided their opponents for believing a rock song could inspire its listeners to murder. "Entertainment is about fantasy and escapism," asserted ACLU chair Danny Goldberg (1992) in a *Los Angeles Times* column: "literalism has nothing to do with entertainment" (p. M2). Goldberg's thesis is founded in the timeworn axiom "it's only a representation," a justification that rings somewhat hollow in an alleged age of Baudrillardian "hyperreality."

Another common tactic used by Ice-T's supporters was to artic- 42 ulate *Body Count* with "legitimate" (i.e., white) art. Writers, including David Hershey-Webb (1995) and Jon Pareles (1992b), decontextualized "Cop Killer"'s black American origins and specificity by placing the song within American culture's "long-established anti-authoritarian streak that often casts the police as symbols of oppression" (Pareles 1992b, C13). Likewise, Barbara Ehrenreich (1992) and Chuck Philips (1992c) invoke rock heroes Bob Dylan, the Beatles, the Rolling Stones "and the other '60s icons who stormed the gates of the Establishment" (Philips 1992c, Calendar 6). "Look, white artists wrote anti-Establishment songs, too," these pundits seem to argue, using a kind of logic easily adaptable for those who wished to associate "Cop Killer" with more commonly denigrated white forms of entertainment. Ehrenreich (1992), Andrew Rosenthal (1992), and Ice-T himself (Philips 1992d) duly noted that neither Dan Quayle nor George Bush saw fit to condemn the cop-killing character played by Bush supporter Arnold Schwarzenegger in *The Terminator* and *Terminator 2: Judgment Day*, while Pareles (1992a) blasted police associations for failing to call for a boycott of "any of the Warner film studio's so-called 'body count' movies." While Pareles's intent may have been to simply bring about a more level playing field, his articulation of "Cop Killer" and Schwarzenegger shoot-em-ups furthers the wrenching of Ice-T's words from their social context.

The most consistent tactic used to support Ice-T's right to express 43 the sentiments of "Cop Killer" was the invocation of his rights under the First Amendment. Employed so frequently that it served as the discursive counterpart to the opposition's corporate ethics articulation, the freedom-of-speech defense was first established by Time Warner in its initial "official" response to the CLEAT boycott: "Time Warner is committed to the free expression of ideas for all our authors, journalists, recording artists, screenwriters, actors and directors. We believe this commitment is crucial to a democratic society, where the full range of opinion and thought—whether we agree with it or not—must be able to find an outlet" (Philips 1992a). The mainstream news media immediately took the bait Time Warner had set: Peter Jennings (1992) defined the "Cop Killer" furor as a "freedom of speech" story on the June 19 telecast of *World News Tonight*. The recording industry and civil liberties groups rallied around Time Warner on these grounds. The president of Capitol Records/EMI Music informed the *Los Angeles Times* that "when you realize that this giant multibillion-dollar corporation is taking a free-speech stand on a record that barely sold a few hundred thousand copies, there can be only one reason why they're holding their ground. It's a matter of principle" (Philips 1992c, 77). The call to ban "Cop Killer" became, to some extent, a free speech issue for Ice-T as well; in the altered version of the album sold by Time Warner starting in August, the First

Amendment appears in place of the printed lyrics to "Cop Killer" in the *Body Count* cassette inset and CD booklet.

The freedom-of-speech defense for "Cop Killer" is deficient in 44 many ways, not the least of which is how its use seemed to endorse the defense of the work only on these grounds. Editorials in both *Billboard* and the *Los Angeles Times* lamented that ink had to be spilled in defense of a song "repugnant . . . to most law-abiding citizens," an "artless and mediocre effort" ("Body Count: The Issue Is Censorship" 1992; "Outrage and Ice-T" 1992); the *Times* reminded Time Warner that "while Americans highly value their strong First Amendment rights, they weary of the Constitution being trotted out to justify any hate-filled, titillating venom that hits the airwaves or bookstores" ("Outrage and Ice-T" 1992). This kind of rhetoric—used to oppose a ban on "Cop Killer"—perhaps influenced Ice-T's later thoughts on the controversy:

> I didn't need anybody to come and say I had the fight to say it. I needed people with credibility to step up and say, "Ice-T not only has the fight to say it, but also fuck the police! . . . We're not apologizing to you cops for what YOU'VE been doing. It's time for people to get angry along with the guy who wrote "Cop Killer." (Ice-T and Siegmund 1994, 171)

Finally, the defenders of Ice-T must share responsibility with the 45 voices of the Right for the evacuation of considerations of hybridity, or "genre crossing" in regard to *Body Count* and "Cop Killer." The interface of cultures represented by Ice-T's thrash-metal experiment was "the unmentionable" in the debate, as neither side wished to engage the implications of the mix of frequently segregated "black" and "white" cultures.

The discourse of gangsta rap is emblematic of our historical 46 period, one in which the power bloc (to borrow Gramsci's term) is relatively insecure and in crisis. American society in the 1990s is characterized by heterogeneity and assimilation, brought about by economic and demographic shifts. Adding to white uncertainty is the effort by subordinated peoples to force the nation to face up to its racial divisions. The racially polarized, discursive fallout from the Rodney King beating, the L.A. rebellion, and the O.J. Simpson trial have encouraged some quarters of white America to locate the problems of American society outside the (figurative and literal) borders of "whiteness."

The significance of rap within this social climate is enormous. Rap 47
is, in Rose's (1994, 100) paraphrasing of James Scott, "a hidden tran-
script . . . [using] cloaked speech and disguised cultural codes to comment on and challenge aspects of current power inequalities." White
anxieties over these distinctly black recodings of hostility and resentment are given expression through the deracialized attacks on rap
music and artists by pundits such as David Samuels (1991). Samuels's
"exposé" of rap's young white audience instead exposes the white fear
of black cultural infiltration, the targets of which are white children.

Blacks justifiably fear that white audiences and manufacturers 48
may "steal" black culture through the increasing commodification of
rap. Nevertheless, Ice-T's incursion into white rock and roll should
be seen, rather than a concession to white interests, as the tactical
theft of white culture. There is a crucial difference: whereas whites
have long appropriated black cultural forms (including rhythm and
blues, the site of rock and roll's origin) for the sake of profit, *Body
Count'* counterappropriation—though it also makes money—serves
to break down the barriers that help segment American culture into
white and black contingents. Ice-T was very much aware of the
alarms his cultural miscegenation would set off; in his *Rolling Stone*
interview, he noted how *Body Count* "got inside suburbia a little
deeper than a normal rap record would. . . . I think by being rock it
infiltrated the homes of a lot of parents not used to having their kids
play records by rappers" (Light 1992b, 30). In the same article, Ice-T
estimated that "ninety-nine percent of the *Body Count* fans are
white"—a hyperbolic statement, perhaps, but one that matches in
spirit the press accounts of the racial breakdown of *Body Count* album
sales and the nearly all-white audiences at the band's live shows
(Light 1992b, 31; Muller 1992; Cusolito 1992).

Through the use of the thrash-metal format, Ice-T designed the 49
Body Count album to be heard by an audience whose racial composition he understood from his band's experience on the 1991
Lollapalooza tour. This complicates our understanding of the lyrics
to "Cop Killer"; Kochman's (1981) work on fighting words does not
readily apply to a case in which blacks, in their own accent, speak to
whites. This point is absolutely essential for a deeper appreciation of
what Ice-T attempted to pull off with his rock band. In disseminating
"white" music with a black accent, *Body Count*—to a greater degree
than Ice-T's rap material—teaches the suburban white teenager
about social conditions far outside of his or her lived experience: a
project of extreme importance in an increasingly multicultural,
multidiscursive age.

In nearly all of the many interviews Ice-T granted in the year of 50
"Cop Killer," the rapper expresses his insistence that white America
learn to listen to its ghettoized black counterpart. For Ice, rap's popularity with suburban white teens is not a cause for concern but a
cause for hope: "They're saying: 'Hold up, these rappers are talking
to me, and it's making me understand. Why did John Wayne always
win? Weren't we taking that land from the Indians? Haven't we been
kind of fucked-up to people?' They're starting to figure it out" (Light
1992a, 17). *The Ice Opinion*, Ice-T writes,

> We are entering a renaissance period, an educational revolution,
> where people are questioning the lies. . . . Our country can't run off
> lies for much longer. The key to keeping the lies alive for the racists
> was the elimination of communication. They kept saying, "Don't
> let them communicate. Don't let them talk to each other. They'll
> never know how much they have in common." (Ice-T and
> Siegmund 1994, 137)

The upshot of David Samuels's (1991) argument in the *New* 51
Republic is that white rap fans use their interaction with "hard" black
culture as a substitute for "real," meaningful social interaction with
blacks (and, presumably, assistance in the alleviation of black
poverty). This conclusion is used as a club by Samuels to discredit all
whites who enjoy hard-core black music: that is, white fandom does
nothing to address the real problem; it only exempts you from it.
Rose (1994, 4) provides a useful corrective to the Samuels position in
Black Noise: "To suggest that rap is a black idiom that prioritizes black
culture and that articulates the problems of black urban life does not
deny the pleasure and participation of others." Whereas Samuels's
view, ironically, ridicules white "cultural tourism" without suggesting a constructive alternative, Rose's view illuminates the possibility
that the mixing of black and white culture may educate America,
teaching us that social struggle in the late twentieth century must be
a partnership. It is a lesson embedded in the hybridity of Ice-T's
music and one we should not soon forget.

References

Agreda, Ann Latham. 1992. An artist reflects society. *Los Angeles
Times,* 10 August, F4.
Bernard, James. 1992. The L.A. rebellion: Message behind the mad-
ness. *The Source,* August, 38–48.

Body Count. 1992a. Cop killer. *On* Body Count. Sire/Warner Bros. Records.

————. 1992b. Out in the parking lot. *On* Body Countf. Sire/Warner Bros. Records.

Body Count: The issue is censorship. 1992. *Billboard*, 18 July, 4.

Bowman, James. 1992. Plain brown rappers. *National Review*, 20 July, 36–38, 53.

Count rises on dealer Body Count ban. 1992. *Billboard*, 18 July, 3, 74.

Cusolito, Karen. 1992. Ice-T tells WB to kill "Cop." *The Hollywood Reporter*, 29 July.

Donnelly, Sally B. 1992. The fire around the Ice. *Time*, 22 June, 66–68.

Duffy, Thom, and Charlene Orr. 1992. Texas police protest Ice-T song. *Billboard*, 20 June, 98.

Ehrenreich, Barbara. 1992. . . Or is it creative freedom? *Time*, 20 July, 89.

Fiske, John. 1996. *Media matters*. Minneapolis: University of Minnesota Press.

Goldberg, Danny. 1992. By taking today's pop culture literally, critics miss the point of entertainment. *Los Angeles Times*, 28 June, M2, M6.

Hall, Stuart. 1980. Gramsci's relevance for the study of race and ethnicity. *Journal of Communication Inquiry* 20 (2): 5–27.

————. 1986. On postmodernism and articulation: An interview with Stuart Hall. *Journal of Communication Inquiry* 10 (2): 45–60.

Hershey-Webb, David. 1995. Number one, with a bullet: Songs of violence are part of America's folk tradition. In *Rap on rap: Straight-up talk on hip-hop culture*, edited by Adam Sexton, 100–6. New York: Delta.

Heston, Charlton. 1992. Heston speaks for women. *Los Angeles Times*, 3 August, F4.

Ice Cube. 1991. Black Korea. *On* Death Certificate. Priority Records.

Ice-T, and Heidi Siegmund. 1994. *The Ice opinion: Who gives a fuck?* New York: St. Martin's.

Jennings, Peter, anchor. 1992. *World News Tonight with Peter Jennings*, ABC, 19 June.

Kelly, Robin D. G. 1996. Kickin' reality, kickin' ballistics: Gangsta rap and postindustrial Los Angeles. In *Droppin' science: Critical essays on rap music and hip hop culture*, edited by William Eric Perkins, 117–58. Philadelphia: Temple University Press.

Kinsley, Michael. 1992. Ice-T: Is the issue social responsibility . . . *Time*, 20 July, 88.

Kochman, Thomas. 1981. *Black and white styles in conflict*. Chicago: University of Chicago Press.

Kuehl, Sheila James. 1992. Ice-T critics miss the rapper's real target. *Los Angeles Times*, 27 July, F3.

Layne, Barry. 1992. Quayle, black cops blast "Killer." *The Hollywood Reporter*, 22 June.

Leo, John. 1992. Rap music's toxic fringe. *U.S. News & World Report*, 29 June, 19.

Light, Alan. 1992a. Rappers sounded warning. *Rolling Stone*, 9-23 July, 15-17.

———. 1992b. Ice-T: The Rolling Stone interview. *Rolling Stone*, 20 August, 28–32, 60.

Mills, David. 1992. Sister Souljah's call to arms. *Washington Post*, 13 May, B1, B4.

Momma dearest. 1992. *New Republic*, 10 August, 7.

Morris, Chris. 1992a. TV a platform for rappers' reactions to riot as Ice-T, Chuck D, MC Ren, others speak out. *Billboard*, 16 May, 65.

———. 1992b. The spotlight turns to freedom in the arts: Police, Time Warner face off over "Cop Killer." *Billboard*, 25 July, 1, 71.

———. 1992c. "Cop" removal satisfies foes, to a point. *Billboard*, 8 August, 1, 83.

Muller, Judy, correspondent. 1992. *World News Tonight with Peter Jennings*, ABC, 24 July.

Outrage and Ice-T: What is the responsibility of the artist? 1992. *Los Angeles Times*, 4 August, B6.

Pareles, Jon. 1992a. Dissing the rappers is fodder for the sound bite. *The New York Times*, 28 June, sec. 2, 20.

———. 1992b. The disappearance of Ice-T's "Cop Killer." *The New York Times*, 30 July, C13, C16.

Philips, Chuck. 1992a. Texas police calls for boycott of Time Warner. *Los Angeles Times*, 12 June, F7.

———. 1992b. Police groups urge halt of record's sale. *Los Angeles Times*, 16 June, F1.

———. 1992c. The uncivil war. *Los Angeles Times*, 19 July, Calendar 6, 76, 77.

———. 1992d. A q&a with Ice-T about rock, race and the "Cop Killer" furor. *Los Angeles Times*, 19 July, Calendar 7.

Pollack, Phyllis. 1992. Uninformed media serve Ice-T bashers' aims. *Billboard*, 11 July, 4.

Quayle, congressmen, L.A. polls join "Cop Killer" posse. 1992. *Billboard*, 4 July, 1, 83.

Rapper Ice-T defends song against spreading boycott. 1992. *The New York Times*, 19 June, C24.

Rose, Tricia. 1994. *Black noise: Rap music and black culture in contemporary America*. Hanover, NH: University Press of New England/Wesleyan University Press.

Rosenthal, Andrew. 1992. Bush denounces rap recording and gives D'Amato a hand. *The New York Times*, 30 June, A21.

Royko, Mike. 1995. A different story if it were "Exec Killer." In *Rap on rap: Straight-up talk on hip-hop culture*, edited by Adam Sexton, 173–76. New York: Delta.

Rule, Sheila. 1992. Rapping Time Warner's knuckles. *The New York Times*, 8 July, C15-C16.

Run on Ice-T's album. 1992. *The New York Times*, 30 July, C16.

Samuels, David. 1991. The rap on rap. *New Republic*, November, 24–29.

Sandow, Greg. 1992. Fire and Ice. *Entertainment Weekly*, 14 August, 30.

Shaw, Bella, anchor. 1992. Ice-T appears on "Arsenio" to discuss controversy. *CNN Showbiz Today*, 22 July.

Trent, Andrea D. 1992. Cops not constructive. *Billboard*, 8 August, 6.

Vice president calls corporation wrong for selling rap song. 1992. *The New York Times*, 20 June, 9.

Volosinov, V. N. 1973. *Marxism and the philosophy of language*. New York: Seminar Press.

Walters, Paul M. 1992. Ice-T's "Cop Killer" can't be justified. *Los Angeles Times* (Orange County ed.), 8 July, B11.

While Time Warner counts its money, America may count its murdered cops (advertisement). 1992. *USA Today*, 26 June, 9A.

White, Timothy. 1991. Editorial. *Billboard*, 23 November, 8.

Will, George F. 1990. America's slide into the sewer. *Newsweek*, 30 July, 64.

Author's note: I would like to extend my appreciation to my colleagues from Professor John Fiske's media events seminar at the University of Wisconsin-Madison, spring 1997, for their helpful comments and suggestions regarding the first draft of this article. In particular, I wish to thank Doug Battema, John Fiske, Jennifer Fuller, Elana Levine, and Jennifer Wang.

Born in Fire: A Hip-Hop Odyssey

Jeff Chang

During the summer of 1975, the South Bronx was burning. New 1
York City officials admitted that they couldn't battle all the fires, let
alone investigate their origins. Chaos reigned. One long hot day in
June, 40 fires were set in a three-hour period.

These were not the fires of purifying rage that ignited Watts in 2
1965, Newark in 1967, or St. Louis and a half dozen other U.S. cities
after the assassination of Martin Luther King, Jr. These were the fires
of abandonment.

As hip-hop journalist S.H. Fernando notes, the Bronx had been a 3
borough of promise for African American, Puerto Rican, Irish, Italian
and Jewish families after World War II. But as industry moved north
to the suburbs during the sixties, housing values collapsed and
whites fled, leaving a population overwhelmingly poor and of
colour.

So slumlords were employing young thugs to systematically 4
burn the devalued buildings to chase out the poor tenants and collect
millions in insurance. Hip-hop, it could be said, was born in fire.

As rapper Grandmaster Flash and the Furious Five's "The 5
Message" would describe it, the New York ghettoes that fuelled hip-
hop's re-creative project were spaces of state neglect and fading liberal dreams. "Got a bum education," the narrator rhymed,
"double-digit inflation, can't take a train to work there's a strike at
the station." But these would also be spaces of spiritual and creative
renewal.

In an earlier era, say the 1920s and 30s when jazz legends like 6
Charles Mingus grew up, a youth might find an extended web of
peers, mentors, patrons, bands and venues through which he or she
might master an instrument and find a vocation. But by the late
1970s, such music education was a luxury for most families.

Jamaican Connection

The result? Play, as African American author Robin D.G. Kelley 7
has put it, became an alternate form of work for a new generation.
Adapting the Jamaican tradition of outdoor dance parties to the grid
and grit of New York, young black and Puerto Rican entrepreneurs

illegally plugged their stereo systems into street light power supplies, and started the party.

With vinyl grooves as sheet music, and a rig of two turntables, a 8 mixer and an amplifier as instruments, Black Art began reinventing itself in 1974 and 1975. That's when a Jamaican immigrant disc jockey named Kool Herc started gaining a reputation in the Bronx for filling the smoky air with "the breaks"—that portion of the song, often as short as two seconds, where the singer dropped out and let the band immerse itself in the groove.

Punching back and forth between two copies of the same 9 record's breaks, then ratcheting up the excitement by shifting to ever more intense breaks, DJs like Herc and Afrika Bambaataa were creating a new aesthetic, which simultaneously satiated and teased the audience.

Escaping the Chaos on the Streets

On the one hand, a loop (of beats) became a metaphor for free- 10 dom: through movement, dancers stretched within the space sculpted by the break. A new canon of songs—drawn from funk, disco, rock, jazz, Afrobeat and reggae—launched new, athletic forms of dancing, which would become known as breakdancing or b-boying. Rather than being passive spectators, the audience engaged in a real dialogue with the disc jockey.

The New York DJs began employing MCs—masters of cere- 11 mony—to affirm the crowd's response to proven breaks, win them over to new breaks, divert them during bad records and generally keep spirits high. In time, the MCs became attractions in their own right. Rocking memorized poems ("writtens") or improvising them on the spot ("freestyles"), the MC became Everyman, the representative of the audience onstage. They reacted to the MC's flow, laughed at his cleverness, cheered his braggadocio, thrilled at his tall-tale spinning, felt his bluesy pain, riding the riddims with words (or "rapping").

The Black Arts poets, the Black Panther messiahs and other rev- 12 olutionary firebrands sharpened their words into spears to attack. This new generation of rappers let the words flow generously, in search of a moment that might serve as a shield of protection, or a transcendent escape from the chaos on the streets.

Popular culture in America is one space where the trope (expres- 13 sion) of working-class creativity is still firmly lodged. American markets are good at providing poor audiences of colour easy access to goods such as music, video and clothing. In the last three decades, a whole class of middlemen entrepreneurs have made fortunes by charting the rapidly shifting terrain of black and brown ghetto chic.

By the late 70s, black and Jewish record label owners in Harlem 14 noted the popularity of hip-hop and rushed to record leading crews. Basically, these owners were geographically and personally close to the music. When a novelty record by the Sugar Hill Gang, "Rapper's Delight" became a surprise international smash, major labels began sniffing around uptown for the next hit. In 1980, Kurtis Blow released rap's first full-length album on a major label. The stage was set for the ascendance of hip-hop culture into the most powerful international youth culture of the late twentieth century.

Until the late 80s, the undisputed centre of this culture was New 15 York. The visual signifiers were provided by the vibrant graffiti movement, whose young renegade artists braved electrified razor-wire fences and armed Metropolitan Transit Authority guards to apply bright spraypaint hieroglyphics onto the city's subways. Every time a train pulled into a station, hip-hop was in respectable society's face, like a middle-finger.

Remember the backdrop to the 1980s: the Reagan administration 16 was launching an attack on the "welfare state", wiping out subsidies for the poor, allowing housing agencies to become dens of corruption while closing down entire categories of government programmes. Hip-hoppers were on the counter-offensive. As the Furious Five warned: "Don't push me 'cause I'm close to the edge. I'm trying not to lose my head. It's like a jungle sometimes, it makes me wonder how I keep from going under."

On the technological front, hip-hoppers racked up one break- 17 through after another. While most rock musicians of the mid-80s were perplexed by new sampling technology, rap producers were turning their new toys into unrelentingly dense, reflexive grooves. Then, as the anti-apartheid movement crested in the U.S., groups like Boogie Down Productions and Public Enemy extended rap's social realism into broader discussions of political action.

But the lofty views of revolutionary nationalism and hardrock 18 spiritualism veered back to the streets in 1989. A group of barely twenty-somethings, who not so ironically called themselves Niggas With Attitude, released what would become an anthem for a generation, *Gangsta Gangsta*. Within six weeks of its release, the album went "gold", selling over 500,000 copies. Hip-hop shot itself into the heart of world culture.

The album, *Straight Outta Compton*, decentered hip-hop from 19
New York to Los Angeles. By the middle of the Reagan administration, Compton was one of a growing number of inner-city nexuses
where deindustrialization, devolution, the cocaine trade, gang structures and rivalries, arms profiteering and police brutality combined
to destabilize poor communities. Chaos was settling in for a long stay
and gangsta rap would be the soundtrack. By conflating myth and
place, the narratives could take root in every 'hood (neighbourhood).
From Portland to Paris, every 'hood could be Compton; everyone
had a story to tell, a cop to fight, a rebellion to launch.

Ironically, gangsta tales populated with drunken, high, rowdy, 20
irresponsible, criminal, murderous "niggas"—its practitioners
likened it to journalism and called it "reality rap"—seemed to be just
what suburbia wanted. As student populations diversified, youth
were increasingly uninterested in whitewashed cultural hand-me-
downs. The 1988 advent of the MTV show, "Yo MTV Raps", made
African American, Chicano, and Latino urban style instantly accessible across the world. With its claims to street authenticity, its teen
rebellion, its extension of urban stereotype and its individualist "get
mine" credo, gangsta rap fit hand-in-glove with a generation weaned
on racism and Reaganism. These were not the old Negro spirituals of
the civil rights era. They were raw, violent, undisciplined, offensive,
"niggafied" rhymes, often homophobic, misogynistic.

Gangsta rap drew new lines in the culture wars. As the music 21
crossed over to whiter, more affluent communities, gangsta rap
inflamed cultural conservatives like Bob Dole and neoliberals like C.
Delores Tucker into demanding new corporate and state repression.
Gangsta rap was even showing up in presidential debates.

Progressives often speculate that gangsta rap was foisted on a 22
young public by reactionary record labels. But to a great extent, the
rise of these popcultural trends was completely unplanned. Well into
the 1990s, major recording labels had no idea what kind of hip-hop
would sell. Unlike rock music, which had long before matured into a
stable and culturally stale economy, hip-hop was like a wild child
whose every gesture and motion was a complete surprise.

In the wake of the Los Angeles riots after the brutal police beat- 23
ing of motorist Rodney King in 1991, gangsta rap and hip-hop
marched toward their greatest commercial success. Dr. Dre's album
The Chronic topically moved gangsta rap away from ghetto commentary to druggy hedonism, and, with its polished chrome sound, onto
mainstream radio playlists. As cast by MTV and the expanding hip-

hop press, artists such as the late Tupac Shakur, the son of a Black Panther revolutionary, made rebellion less a battle in the culture wars, and ever more a mere marker of youth style.

The shrinking music industry also transformed the hip-hop 24 scene. Between the early to mid-90s, several of the independent record label owners who had been instrumental in launching the music sold their companies to major labels, which also began consolidating and reducing the size of their rosters. As a result, grassroots acts no longer went from the streets to the top of the charts. Management firms guaranteed polished stars and funded the farm teams that would take those stars' places in turn. The new hip-hop sound, crisply digitized and radio-ready, became mainstream pop.

With the massive major label distribution juggernauts behind 25 them, it became routine for the biggest hip-hop acts to debut with gold (half-million) or more sales. A half-dozen magazines were launched to take advantage of the new wealth of advertising dollars. Hollywood's big money came calling, making multimedia stars of rappers LL Cool J and Ice Cube. Commercial tie-ins with products such as Sprite or the Gap clothing proliferated for second-level artists. Producer Russell Simmons began calling the hip-hop generation "the biggest brand-building generation the world has ever seen". The audience had matured into a marketable demographic.

Rebellion or Capitulation?

As U.S. author Don DeLillo has written, "Capital burns off the 26 nuance in a culture." To be sure, hip-hop has transformed popular culture across the world. In Kenya, youngsters wear Adidas baseball caps, Nike shoes and stage rowdy rap concerts that look like versions of Bambaataa's romps in the Bronx of yore. It's unclear whether such performances reflect a hybrid youth rebellion or capitulation to global capitalism.

Yet somewhere within the culture lies the key to understanding 27 an entire generation. This culture forged in fire still keeps its hand near the match. Rap rewards those who "represent" its audiences' realities. If this often appears as caving in to baser impulses, hip-hop's defense is that it speaks to young people as they are and where they are.

And yet a growing movement believes that the culture is liberat- 28 ing. In cities across the world, youths use hip-hop to organise the struggles against racism, police brutality, and the prison-industrial complex. For them, the culture and the politics are inseparable—they are all part of a cohesive world-view. Therein finally lies the story: hip-hip, born of the destructive fires of the 1960s and 70s, has rekindled creative flames of hope in a new generation. The cleansing fires are still to come.

Understanding Youth, Popular Culture, and the Hip-Hop Influence

Patricia Thandi Hicks Harper

America's youth represent a distinct group with their own 1
unique popular culture—a culture within which Hip-Hop recurrently permeates.

Despite adult attitudes (both positive and negative) about youth 2
culture, we know we must have a working knowledge of this culture
that engulfs and contextualizes our young people's lives if we are to
effectively communicate with them. It is important to understand the
information that they process. The rules of social marketing are pertinent and suggest that effective communication begins with knowing your target audience.

Collectively, youth in America represent a powerful movement 3
that transcends race, ethnicity, gender, and social or economic status.
America's youth are a walking depiction of their worldview that is
externally manifested through clothing, art, attitude, style, movement, music, video, television, film, language, and the World Wide
Web.

Youth are big business, and everyone is struggling for their atten- 4
tion: advertisers; large and small businesses; media conglomerates;
the sports, fashion, and entertainment industries; faith communities;
health arenas; schools; community-based organizations; families;
and even local, state, and federal governments.

Many of America's youth need adult assistance, nurturing, 5
supervision, and resources because they are at-risk for making negative and harmful behavioral choices. Those entities that will succeed
in reaching these young people with their messages or products are
those who are the most culturally competent in youth popular culture and who use this knowledge and experience as a foundation for
their education and information dissemination outreach strategies.

The need for cultural competence in understanding and appreci- 6
ating racial and ethnic diversity is well recognized in corporate, community, and governmental arenas. The influx of international racial
and ethnic groups over the past 20 years has made it necessary for
America to develop communication efforts that are targeted, authentic, culturally sensitive, and designed to speak appropriately to cultural nuances.

Yet, America has not voiced the same urgency in understanding   7
the culture of youth. It is time that we understood that culture is not
limited to race, ethnicity, gender, or sexuality. Programs targeting
youth must demonstrate a sensitivity to and an understanding of
young people and their design for living and interpreting their environment.

By examining youth culture, we can form a guide for predicting   8
behavioral choices and for determining the strategies necessary to
change and influence those choices.

Youth Popular Culture Competence

Youth popular culture is simply defined as that which is "in,"   9
contemporary, and has the stamp of approval of young people. It is
that which has mass appeal; it is nonlinear and eclectic. The culture
dictates what become the shared norms that provide young people
"with a deep sense of belonging and often with a strong preference
for behaving in certain ways." It is "psycho-socio-cultural" in that its
primary elements involve the reciprocal interaction of individual,
social, and cultural forces.

Youth popular culture has aspects that cross racial, ethnic, and   10
geographical boundaries, and while all youth do not behave or think
in the exact same ways, many similarities suggest that the vast majority of adolescents fit somewhere within the mainstream of an
American youth popular culture. How youth spend their time; what
they value; their attitudes, styles, and behaviors; their concerns; and
how they interact with mass mediated messages, their peers, and
society-at-large constitute youth popular culture.

Because our mass popular culture is the most influential in the   11
world, youth, as the drivers of the culture, are very powerful. While
some scholars maintain that today's youth are extremely diverse in
terms of their culture (whether they be heroes, nerds, urban martyrs,
or valley girls), we contend that the strength of youth popular culture
today is in what young people have in common with each other. The
challenge for health professionals, educators, and others who intend
to effectively communicate with youth is to get a good read on what
is happening within this culture and to recognize the commonalities.
The key, again, is to become and/or remain youth popular culture
competent.

The U.S. Department of Health and Human Services' Center for   12
Substance Abuse Prevention (CSAP) defines cultural competence as:

A set of academic and interpersonal skills that allow individuals to increase their understanding and appreciation of cultural differences and similarities within, among, and between groups. This requires a willingness and ability to draw on community-based values, traditions, and customs and to work with knowledgeable persons of and from the community in developing focused interventions, communications, and other supports.

CSAP stresses the importance of cultural competence for effec- 13 tively maximizing substance abuse prevention and intervention efforts. The point is that health professionals, educators, and anyone else targeting youth must honestly address the following questions:

- "How well do I really know the target audience?"

- "How much do I really know about their racial, ethnic, and adolescent culture?"

- "How much do I really understand about their worldview and how they interact within society?"

- "How much do I really know about how young people use media?"

- "How important is it for me to be culturally competent about youth popular culture?"

- "Do I base my responses on newly obtained information about today's youth culture, or do I make judgments based on speculation or the opinions of others and/or media?"

Once these questions are addressed, the knowledge, under- 14 standing, and appreciation gaps must be filled. The related issues must be explored by taking the most appropriate actions (based on the definition), which will lead to increased cultural competence. The result would be more effective communication with youth populations because health professionals and educators would be more cognizant of their psycho-socio-cultural realities. Communication would be more directly targeted.

A 17-year-old female living in an urban area of Washington, DC, 15 describes effective communication from her perspective. She states:

Sometimes when young people are being criticized, they get so angry [that] they're not actually listening to what these people have to say. The older generation is not communicating because they're being so critical without really looking and listening. If they would just listen to what matters to us, they might be able to communicate better. We're not that bad. But the younger people have to check themselves too and listen to what the older generation is saying. They do know a lot. Everybody has to listen to each other. Maybe then we'll get on the same page.

We at the Institute maintain that it is imperative for those who 16 work with youth to seriously explore and consider the potential effectiveness of using what we call youth popular culture's inherent and associated "formal features," contexts, and appropriate content for effective communication. We contend that it is important to move beyond society's and professionals' negative associations with the culture and to explicate how its characteristics and attributes can best be utilized in the interest of those who are captivated by it on a daily basis. At the same time, we know we must clarify that we are not implying that anyone should give his or her blessing to all aspects of youth popular culture or that anyone should encourage an unexamined conformism by young people.

The Formal Features

Formal features are those elements that give communicative 17 strength to messages and are usually discussed within the context of visual media. The formal features of youth popular culture, for purposes of this article, include elements and characteristics that can be manifested through all media and personal communication.

The role that youth popular culture's formal features play in the 18 everyday lives of youth suggests them as integral factors of youth popular culture. Leading contemporary anthropologist C. P. Kottack discusses the "features" of popular culture, indicating that these "features are sometimes regarded as trivial and unworthy of serious study." We beg to differ, as does Kottack, and contend that ideology, predilection, belief, language, and formal features (which to some degree encompass the other cultural aspects) constitute youth culture—which influences the choices youth make.

The features allow for the shaping and customizing of messages 19 and materials that target youth and that illustrate the creative relationship between distinct styles of form and content. The formal features of youth popular culture provide resourceful pathways for effective and affective communication with target audiences. Examples of these formal features include:

- bold
- "rhythm" driven
- eclectic
- colors
- urban
- non-governmental
- "popular music" driven
- "attitude" driven
- humorous
- power-to-the-youth centered
- family connected
- spiritual
- celebrity-icon driven
- non-linear
- jargon specific
- dance
- "sports" focused
- to the point
- technological
- "keeping it real" driven
- full of verve
- "posse" driven

The formal features of youth popular culture are multidirectional, eclectic, familiar, and nontraditional (compared to European standards of traditional culture, which may be described as linear, hierarchical, standardized, individualistic, and rule-oriented). [20]

The use of these features in designing pro-health and education messages would make a youth's cognitive processing and sanctioning of these messages more likely because of the features' cultural appropriateness and relation to a youth's already existing mental frameworks of prototypical experiences (schemata). [21]

Youth will respond positively to information couched within a   22
cultural context that genuinely acknowledges their worldviews.
Knowledge of youth popular culture's formal features will assist
educators and health professionals:

- in more creatively facilitating their students' learning
  process

- in their efforts to develop and design messages targeting
  youth

- in their efforts to get youth interested about sexuality education and living healthy lifestyles

- in their efforts to effectively communicate using a variety of
  formats

- in enhancing their cultural competence as it relates to youth
  as a cultural group

Hip-Hop Culture

Hip-Hop culture is America's dominant youth popular culture   23
today. This is the reason why adults who target youth must be clear
about it. Hip-Hop is a cultural phenomenon in the American mainstream. Noted writer of popular music culture, Nelson George, suggests that we all exist in what can legitimately be called a "Hip-Hop
America." While some may argue that other youth cultures (e.g.,
Rock and Punk youth culture) are just as pervasive in the lives of
youth, we at the Institute profess that the masses of young people are
engulfed in selected aspects of Hip-Hop and that other popular
youth cultures have embraced its vastness, thereby creating an inter-
change of styles for popularity.

Hip-Hop's legacy lies in the old and ancient traditions of African   24
people, however, its contemporary status has evolved from a subter-
ranean Bronx (NY) expression in the early 1970s to a profitable com-
modity worldwide. The origin of what is now contemporary
Hip-Hop lies in the backyards, basements, and communities of inner-
city Black and Hispanic/Latino youth.

The name Hip-Hop also has a distinct origin. According to R T.   25
Perkins and the nationally and internationally acclaimed founder of
the "Universal Zulu Nation Movement" and "Godfather of Hip-Hop
and Rap" Afrika Bambaataa:

The term Hip-Hop was taken out of verses that Love Bug Starski used to say "to the Hip-Hop you don't stop" and it was the Zulu Nation that took it and named the whole culture Hip-Hop. Hip-Hop is something that's the whole culture, the whole picture of the movement which is the break dancing, the graffiti art, the rapping, the scratching, the deejaying, the style of dress, the lyrics, the way you look, the walk, it's all this combined . . . the attitude.

Hip-Hop is an "all encompassing" culture for many of America's youth. It includes forces that affect and influence the choices these youth make in their everyday lives. Hip-Hop represents a strong and unified youth consciousness; it is a powerful and pervasive movement among youth worldwide. Youth, regardless of who they are or where they come from, very likely will identify with at least some aspect of Hip-Hop culture. [26]

Today, the formal features of Hip-Hop are successfully used to communicate a myriad of messages and to sell products which profitably, ethically, and unethically target the masses of young people. The understanding of Hip-Hop and its influence within popular culture has proven to be very effective for influencing behavioral choices and drawing the attention of young people to various subject areas. An exploration of Hip-Hop music (particularly Rap music) will show that youth of various races and ethnic groups are purchasing the music to significant degrees. Research indicates that white American teens purchase Rap in larger numbers than do their African-American counterparts. "More than 70 percent of Hip-Hop albums are purchased by Whites," all of whom contribute to the fact that the music is now a billion dollar industry. [27]

Rap music continues to lead the way in album sales growth when compared to other music genres (e.g., R & B, Country, Alternative). According to Byran Turner, president and CEO of SoundScan: [28]

> Rap album sales shot up 32 percent in just 12 months, first time. That jump makes for the largest single-year gain by any genre since SoundScan began collecting sales data eight years ago.

Hirschorn, past editor of *Spin* music magazine, compares Hip-Hop and rock music sales data. He supports the argument that "the energy now days is in Hip-Hop" and contends that: [29]

> When Hip-Hop albums as strong as Lauryn Hill's or Outcast's sell as well as they did, it's hard to argue about the quality. The

question is whether rock is going to lose a whole generation of young listeners, who are naturally gravitating to Hip-Hop now.

Hip-Hop's pervasive influence within the fashion, film, television, and dot.com industries clearly show the culture as one of choice for many of America's youth. It is a culture that must not be ignored because of its mainstay status within the American mainstream. It is a culture whose elements must be explored as a useful contextual backdrop for effective communication. (See "Reaching the Hip-Hop Generation with 'Pro-Social' Behavior Messages" in the June-July 1999 issue of the SIECUS Report.) [30]

Cultural Competency in the Classroom

Many of America's educators, regardless of their subject area, still fail to consider culture when determining their teaching methodologies and exploring the best ways to communicate with and to their students. [31]

Consequently, there is an evident lack of cultural responsiveness, relevance, and significance in classroom environment, and too many students remain uninterested and lack the motivation required to process important information. [32]

Those educators who continue to conduct classroom "business as usual"—failing to realize that "traditional approaches to pedagogy have tended to be rigid and uncreative [and that] they are far from exhausting the wonderful possibilities for teaching and learning"—must work hard to take the classroom experience to higher heights by increasing their youth popular culture competence and, therefore, creativity. As a result, their relationships with students will be enhanced; and students will more readily enjoy their learning experience. [33]

Summary and Conclusion

Today's youth popular culture has evolved into a phenomenon much different from what it was 40 years ago. [34]

Unlike the days of *Ozzie & Harriet*, when youth listened to one popular radio station and looked forward to the annual school dance, many of today's youth are taking risque spring breaks at summer resorts; going to clubs that cater to adult audiences; participating in gang-related activities; surfing the Net; experiencing peer pressure to [35] use drugs and to have sexual relationships; choosing from over 100 television channels and at least four popular radio stations; having direct access to images of pornography, violence, and drug-use live and via broadcast media; and much more.

Given these realities, and in order to stimulate critical thinking, influence attitudes and behaviors, and maintain the attention, curiosity, and interest of today's young generation, we need a revolution in the way that health and education-related information and messages are designed and delivered. We must supplement our traditional communication strategies with ones that are more sensitive to the worldviews of our youth. 36

Hip-Hop culture can be convincingly argued to be the leading force within youth popular culture nationwide. It is the pipeline for effectively communicating to and with young people. The pipeline connects to the mental, social, and cultural tenets of the vast majority of America's youth. As legendary rapper, activist, and author Chuck D puts it: for many young people Hip-Hop is their CNN. 37

It is my hope that this article will stimulate professional dialogue around the related issues and that all of us will focus even more thoroughly on increasing our youth popular culture competence in an effort to enhance and improve our relationships and communication targeting this very vulnerable population. 38

4

TECHNOLOGY

WE ARE NOT SPECIAL

Rodney A. Brooks

If we accept evolution as the mechanism that gave rise to us, we 1
understand that we are nothing more than a highly ordered collection of biomolecules. Molecular biology has made fantastic strides over the last fifty years, and its goal is to explain all the peculiarities and details of life in terms of molecular interactions. A central tenet of molecular biology is that *that is all there is*. There is an implicit rejection of mind-body dualism, and instead an implicit acceptance of the notion that mind is a product of the operation of the brain, itself made entirely of biomolecules. We will look at these statements in more detail later in the chapter. So every living thing we see around us is made up of molecules—biomolecules plus simpler molecules like water.

All the stuff in people, plants, and animals comes from trans- 2
cription of DNA into proteins, which then interact with each other to produce structure and other compounds. Food, drink, and breath are also taken into the bodies of these organisms, and some of that may get directly incorporated into the organism as plaque or other detritus. The rest of it either reacts directly with the organism's biomolecules and is broken down into standard components—simple biomolecules or elements that bind to existing biomolecules—or is rejected and excreted. Thus almost everything in the body is biomolecules.

Biomolecules interact with each other according to well-defined   3
laws. As they come together in any particular orientation, there are
electrostatic forces at play that cause them to deform and physically
interact. Chemical processes may be initiated that cause one or both
of the molecules to cleave in interesting ways. With the totality of
molecules, even in a single cell, there are chances for hundreds or
thousands of different intermolecular reactions. It is impossible then
to know or predict exactly which molecules will react with which
other ones, but a statistical model of the likelihood of each type of
reaction can be constructed. From that we can say whether a cell will
grow, or whether it provides the function of a neuron, or whatever.

The body, this mass of biomolecules, is a machine that acts   4
according to a set of specifiable rules. At a higher level the subsys-
tems of the machine can be described in mechanical terms also. For
instance, the liver takes in certain products, breaks them down, and
recycles them. The details of how it operates can be divined from the
particular bioreactions that go on within it, but only a few of those
reactions are important to the liver itself. The vast majority of them
are the normal housekeeping reactions that are in almost every cell in
the body.

The body consists of components that interact according to well-   5
defined (though not all known to us humans) rules that ultimately
derive from physics and chemistry. The body is a machine, with perhaps billions of billions of parts, parts that are well ordered in the
way they operate and interact. We are machines, as are our spouses,
our children, and our dogs.

Needless to say, many people bristle at the use of the word   6
"machine." They will accept some description of themselves as col-
lections of components that are governed by rules of interaction, and
with no component beyond what can be understood with mathematics, physics, and chemistry. But that to me is the essence of what
a machine is, and I have chosen to use that word to perhaps brutal-
ize the reader a little. . . . The particular material of which we are
made may be different. Our physiology may be vastly different, but
at heart I am saying we are much like the robot Genghis, although
somewhat more complex in quantity but not in quality. This is the
key loss of specialness with which I claim mankind is currently faced.

And why the bristling at the word "machine"? Again, it is the   7
deep-seated desire to be special. To be more than mere. The idea that
we are machines seems to make us have no free will, no spark, no life.
But people seeing robots like Genghis and Kismet do not think of
them as clockwork automatons. They interact in the world in ways

that are remarkably similar to the ways in which animals and people interact. To an observer they certainly seem to have wills of their own.

When I was younger, I was perplexed by people who were both religious and scientists. I simply could not see how it was possible to keep both sets of beliefs intact. They were inconsistent, and so it seemed to me that scientific objectivity demanded a rejection of religious beliefs. It was only later in life, after I had children, that I realized that I too operated in a dual nature as I went about my business in the world.

On the one hand, I believe myself and my children all to be mere machines. Automatons at large in the universe. Every person I meet is also a machine—a big bag of skin full of biomolecules interacting according to describable and knowable rules. When I look at my children, I can, when I force myself, understand them in this way. I can see that they are machines interacting with the world.

But this is not how I treat them. I treat them in a very special way, and I interact with them on an entirely different level. They have my unconditional love, the furthest one might be able to get from rational analysis. Like a religious scientist, I maintain two sets of inconsistent beliefs and act on each of them in different circumstances.

It is this transcendence between belief systems that I think will be what enables mankind to ultimately accept robots as emotional machines, and thereafter start to empathize with them and attribute free will, respect, and ultimately rights to them. Remarkably, to me at least, my argument has turned almost full circle on itself. I am saying that we must become less rational about machines in order to get past a logical hangup that we have with admitting their similarity to ourselves. Indeed, what I am really saying is that we, all of us, overanthropomorphize humans, who are after all mere machines. When our robots improve enough, beyond their current limitations, and when we humans look at them with the same lack of prejudice that we credit humans, then too we will break our mental barrier, our need, our desire, to retain tribal specialness, differentiating ourselves from them. Such leaps of faith have been necessary to overcome racism and gender discrimination. The same sort of leap will be necessary to overcome our distrust of robots.

Resistance Is Futile

If indeed we are mere machines, then we have instances of machines that we all have empathy for, that we treat with respect, that we believe have emotions, that we believe even are conscious. That instance is us. So then the mere fact of being a machine does not disqualify an entity from having emotions. If we really are machines, then in principle we could build another machine out of matter that was identical to some existing person, and it too would have emotions and surely be conscious.

Now the question is how different can we make our 13 Doppelgänger from the original person it was modeled upon. Surely it does not have to be precisely like some existing person to be a thinking, feeling creature. Every day new humans are born that are not identical to any previous human, and yet they grow to be a unique emotional, thinking, feeling creature. So it seems that we should be able to change our manufactured human a little bit and still have something we would all be willing to consider a human. Once we admit to that, we can change things some more, and some more, and perhaps eventually build something out of silicon and steel that is still functionally the same as a human, and thus would be accepted as a human. Or at least accepted as having emotions.

Some would argue that if it was made of steel and silicon, then 14 as long as people did not know that, they might accept it as human. As soon as the secret was out, however, it would no longer be accepted. But that lack of acceptance cannot be on the basis that it is a machine, as we are already supposing that we are machines. Indeed, the many arguments that abound about why a machine can never have real emotions, or really be intelligent, all boil down to a denial of one form or another, that we are machines, or at least machines in the conventional sense.

So here is the crux of the matter. I am arguing that we are 15 machines and we have emotions, so in principle it is possible for machines to have emotions as we have examples of them (us) that do. Being a machine does not disqualify something from having emotions. And, by straightforward extension, does not prevent it from being conscious. This is an assault on our specialness, and many people argue that it cannot be so, and argue that they need to make the case that we are more than machines.

Sometimes they are arguing that we are more than conventional 16 computers. This may well be the case, and I have not, so far, taken any position on this. But I *have* taken a position that we are machines.

ISOLATED BY THE INTERNET

Clifford Stoll

For all my grinching about the soul-deadening effects of the 1
Internet, most Internet users speak positively about it. One friend
tells how she found a support group for an obscure medical condition. Another tells me that his modem provides an escape from a dull
world, providing a rich mixture of fantasy and role playing. One
soon-to-be-married couple writes how they met through postings to
a Usenet news group. And one computer programmer confesses that
although she's extremely shy in person, in her electronic chat room,
she becomes a feisty, enchanting contessa. Meanwhile, wired families
keep in touch via email, and new friendships blossom thanks to
online special interest groups. Isolated hobbyists sign onto Web sites
to exchange information and help each other. Surely the electronic
virtual community is a positive social development.

Well, not necessarily. According to Carnegie Mellon University 2
psychologists Robert Kraut and Vicki Lundmark, there are serious
negative long-term social effects, ranging from depression to loneliness. The result of a concerted research effort, their findings were surprising, since this research was funded by high-tech firms like AT&T,
Apple Computer, Lotus, Intel, and Hewlett-Packard. Their report,
"The Internet Paradox—A Social Technology That Reduces Social
Involvement and Psychological Well-Being?" appeared in the
September 1998 issue of the *American Psychologist*.

Kraut and Lundmark had asked how using the Internet affects 3
connections between people. They looked at both the extent and the
depth of human links, and tried to understand how the Internet
affected these connections. Deep social ties are relationships with frequent contact, deep feelings of involvement, and broad content.
Weak ties have superficial and easily broken bonds, infrequent contact, and narrow focus. Weak ties link us to information and social
resources outside our close local groups. But it's the strong social ties
that buffer us from stress and lead to better social interactions.

Hardly surprising that strong personal ties come about when 4
you're in close proximity to someone . . . it's been that way for millennia. Suddenly, along comes the Internet, reducing the importance

of distance and letting you develop new relationships through chat rooms, email, news groups, and Web pages.

To learn about the social effects of the Internet, Kraut and Lundmark followed ninety-six families of various backgrounds for two years. They provided computers, software, modems, accounts, and training; in all, some 256 individuals entered the study, and two thirds of them completed it. The software allowed full Internet use but recorded how much time was spent in various online activities. Each participant answered questionnaires before they went online, after a year, and after two years of Internet use.

The researchers measured stress, loneliness, and depression using standardized psychological tests like the UCLA Loneliness Scale and the Center for Epidemiologic Studies Depression Scale. Participants would agree or disagree with statements like "I feel everything I do is an effort," "I enjoy life," "I can find companionship when I want it," "There is someone I could turn to for advice about changing my job or finding a new one." Kraut and Lundmark then measured each participant's social circle and distant social network during the two-year study.

After following the study group, the psychologists found an average increase in depression by about 1 percent for every hour spent online per week. Online activity resulted in increased loneliness as well. On the average, subjects began with sixty-six members in their nearby social circle. For every hour each week spent online, this group shrank by about 4 percent.

Depression. Loneliness. Loss of close friendships. This is the medium that we're promoting to expand our global community?

It's true that many online relationships developed as well, but most represented weak social ties rather than deep ones: a woman who exchanged mittens with a stranger, a man who exchanged jokes with a colleague he met over a tourist Web site. A few friendships blossomed—one teenager met his prom date online—but these were rarities. And even though such friendships were welcomed when they happened, there was an overall decline in real-world interaction with family and friends.

The overwhelming majority of online friendships simply aren't deep. Online friends can't be depended on for help with tangible favors: small loans, baby-sitting, help with shopping, or advice about jobs and careers. One participant "appreciated the email correspondence she had with her college-aged daughter, yet noted that when her daughter was homesick or depressed, she reverted to telephone calls to provide support."

Kraut and Lundmark concluded that "greater use of the Internet 11 was associated with small but statistically significant declines in social involvement as measured by communication within the family and the size of people's local social networks, and with increases in loneliness and depression. Other effects on the size of the distant social circle, social support, and stress did not reach standard significance levels but were consistently negative." Paradoxically, the Internet is a social technology used for communication, yet it results in declining social involvement and psychological well-being.

What's important to remember is that their research wasn't a collection of casual claims, but "an extremely careful scientific study," said Tora Bikson, a senior scientist at Rand Corporation. "It's not a result that's easily ignored." Despite a decade of concerns, it's the first time that professional psychologists have done such a longitudinal study.

"We were shocked by the findings, because they are counterintuitive to what we know about how socially the Internet is being used," said Dr. Kraut, who hypothesized that Internet use is "building shallow relationships, leading to an overall decline in feeling of connection to other people."

Not surprisingly, computer makers scoffed: One Intel psychologist replied that "This is not about the technology, per se; it's about how it is used. It points to the need for considering social factors in terms of how you design applications and services for technology." In other words, technology is just a neutral tool and social technologists will solve this problem. Uh, right.

According to computer scientists James Katz and Philip Aspden, there's no reason to be pessimistic about the social effects of Internet use. They telephoned six hundred Internet users to survey the social effects of computer use. Their 1997 report, "A Nation of Strangers," argues that the Internet augments existing communities. It's a medium for creating friendships and to stay in touch with family members. They cheerily suggest that some two million new meetings have taken place thanks to the Internet. Katz and Aspden happily conclude that "The Internet is creating a nation richer in friendships and social relationships."

Unfortunately, Katz and Aspden used a biased system of self-reporting, a phone survey in which those called judged themselves on whether they had gained or lost friends. Hardly anyone's going to tell a stranger on the phone, "Oh, I've lost friends because I spend too much time online." Also, while Katz and Aspden tallied all social ties made over the Internet, they didn't probe into the possible loss of strong local ties. Since they didn't ask about the depth, nature, or quality of online "friendships," naturally their phone survey delivered a happily optimistic conclusion.

Psychologists point out that the best predictor of psychological 17 troubles is a lack of close social contacts. There's a surprisingly close correlation between social isolation and such problems as schizophrenia and depression. Long hours spent online undercut our local social support networks; this isolation promotes psychological troubles.

Kraut and Lundmark's work points to a serious problem loom- 18 ing for wired generations: Will the proliferation of shallow, distant social ties make up for the loss of close local links?

Stanford psychology professor Philip Zimbardo has part of the 19 answer. Since the mid-1970s, he's studied the psychology of shyness. In 1978, Dr. Zimbardo found that some 40 percent of undergraduates said, "I think of myself as shy." By 1988, this number had reached 45 percent. And by 1995, some 50 percent of undergrads saw themselves as shy; some research suggests that 60 percent of the population now suffers from shyness.

Why this epidemic of shyness? At a 1997 conference, Professor 20 Zimbardo pointed to several reasons, many connected to technology. Television and computing make us more passive . . . and passivity feeds into shyness. Now that many family members have separate televisions, watching TV is no longer a communal experience, but rather an isolated, nonsocial nonencounter. One report suggested that parents, busy from work which they've brought home, spend only six to eight minutes a day talking with their children.

"The electronic revolution of emails and faxes means the 21 medium has finally become the message," said Professor Zimbardo. "With more virtual reality overtaking real reality, we're losing ordinary social skills, and common social situations are becoming more awkward."

Yep, for better or worse, the only way to learn how to get along 22 with others is to spend plenty of time interacting with people. Email, telephones, and faxes all prevent us from learning basic skills of dealing with people face to face. These electronic intermediaries dull our abilities to read each other's gestures and facial expressions, to express our feelings, to strike up conversations with strangers, to craft stories, to tell jokes.* Those weaned on computer communica-

---

* Once, people told stories—you'd pay attention to the homegrown comedian who knew how to tell a joke. Joke telling meant timing, inflection, and expression. Now, thanks to jokes passed by email and Internet forums, stale comedy routines constantly circulate online. People who can't tell jokes won't shut their mouths.

tions won't learn basic social rules of conversation. How to interrupt. How to share time with another. How to speak to an audience. When to be quiet.

In the past, shyness has been passed off as a trivial problem that 23 children grow out of. "Although we think of shy people as passive and easily manipulated, at the same time there is a level of resentment, rage, and hostility," Zimbardo warned. I wonder if that explains some of the anger pervading the anonymous chat rooms and postings to Usenet news groups.

The notion that people can become addicted to the Internet was 24 scoffed at by professional psychologists. It was considered to be a joke in the same way that alcoholism, compulsive gambling, and obsessive shopping were thought laughable in the 1950s. After all, you can just stop. Only recently have a few psychologists asked questions about the seductive nature of the Internet and the type of person likely to become hooked. They're finding that the clinical definitions of established addictions fit the profiles of plenty of people who spend their lives online.

Psychologist Kimberly Young was among the first to investigate 25 clinical cases of Internet addiction. She tells of a Pennsylvania college student she calls Steve who's online sixty to seventy hours a week. Steve's a wizard in the Multi-User Dungeons; Internet fantasy games best known as MUDs.

"MUDs are like a religion to me, and I'm a god there. I'm 26 respected by all the other MUDders. . . . Even when I'm not playing, I wonder if there will be more newbies for me to kill that night or which other guys will be playing. I am in control of my character and my destiny in this world. My character is a legend and I identify with him." Yet when Steve's not online, he's held back by low self-esteem. Shy and awkward around people, he's uncomfortable around women and believes he doesn't fit in at school. "When I'm playing the MUDs, I'm not feeling lonely or mopey. I'm not thinking about my problems. . . . I want to stay on the MUDs as long as I possibly can."

Where once Steve would have work within the real world and 27 slowly learn how to deal with people, today he is able to turn to the Internet for solace and escape.

Compounding the withdrawal of individuals from their close 28 social circle, technology also blurs the line between work and play. Thanks to telephones, pagers, and cell phones, work seeps into our private time, forcing shallow, impersonal communication into quiet hours and intimate moments. Email reaches our desktops and laptops; even our wristwatches have alarms and electronic reminders.

At home, on the road, or on the golf course, we can't escape an electronic bombardment.

Walking in Yosemite Park, I met a hiker with all the latest paraphernalia hanging from his belt: pager, GPS locator, and electronic altimeter. Amid the quiet of the sugar pines, his cell phone squawked and I overheard one side of his conversation with some New York advertising firm: "Tell both clients that I won't be able to make Monday's meeting," he told an unseen secretary. "I'll get them a proposal when I'm over this cold." 29

Here's a guy who's brought the stress of his office into the tranquillity of the forest. He's never lost and always in reach. At the same time, he's utterly lost and out of touch.* 30

Office work tags along with homes equipped with fax machines. On the street, drivers and pedestrians dodge each other while talking over cell phones. In cafes, nerds type on laptops. Office managers bring their work home on floppy disks. The telecommuter merely represents one milestone in the blurring of home and office. 31

As work sneaks into playtime, play just isn't as much fun. Used to be that only students brought classwork home; increasingly, everyone has homework, everyone's on call. Our home provides little refuge from the stress of the outside world. 32

This isn't just the fault of technology—so many people want high-tech careers and professions that they willingly latch onto jobs which demand twenty-four-hour availability. And so we find the Webmaster who's on call all night, just in case the file server crashes. The high school teacher who answers students' email all evening. The gardener who polishes her Web site when she comes home. For them, home is simply an extension of their workplace. 33

For children, home computers, instructional videotapes, and educational television extend the school into their home. Forget the innocence of childhood: Our kids are increasingly programmed as academic automatons. 34

The Internet is widely promoted as an aid for speed, profit, productivity, and efficiency. These business goals simply aren't the aims of a home. Maybe there's such a thing as kitchen productivity, but efficiency doesn't make much sense in my living room, and exactly who considers profits in their bedroom? 35

---

* In response to the noise and interruptions, one Japanese symphony hall has installed special transmitters to disable all cell phones and pagers in the audience. I hadn't realized it before, but one of the joys of speleology is that none of my caving partners can be reached a hundred feet under the ground.

At home, our goals might include tranquillity, reflection, and ₃₆ warmth . . . hardly the image brought up by the phrase "home computing." With houses increasingly wired for communications, electronic messages invade our home life. It's not just the telemarketers who disrupt dinner with sales and surveys. Rather, our private space is increasingly available to the outside world, whether it's a call from the boss, tonight's business news on the TV, or an email message about a business meeting.

Nor are the goals of business those of a school. Productivity ₃₇ doesn't map onto a sixth-grade class in pre-algebra. It's absurd to speak of increasing the efficiency of an instructor teaching a third-grade student how salt melts ice. Will a 200-MHz computer educate a child twice as fast as a 100-MHz computer?

The way we communicate constrains how we interact. Computer ₃₈ networks provide chat rooms in which emotions must fit into eighty columns of ASCII text, punctuated by smiley faces. No longer need my correspondent begin a letter with a gratuitous "Dear Cliff." Rather, the header of the email describes recipient, sender, and subject. Any pretense of politeness is erased by the cold efficiency of the medium.

One survey reports that office workers typically receive 190 mes- ₃₉ sages per day. Yet computer network promoters tell us that we need ever faster links and constantly more connectivity. Will I get more work done today if I receive three hundred messages rather than two hundred?

Instead of encouraging me to concentrate on a single job, the con- ₄₀ stant stream of electronic messages makes me constantly flip from one task to another. Computers are great at doing this, but people aren't. Promoters of electronic work-places may speak glowingly of living asynchronous lives, but most of my work requires concentration, thinking, and organization . . . hardly promoted by a river of electronic messages.

Getting a high-speed link to the Internet causes Web pages to ₄₁ load faster. At first glance, you'd think that this would reduce the amount of time that students would spend online. Hardly. As connection speeds increase, college students spend more time surfing the Web and less time writing, studying, or whatever they don't want to do. Same's true for office workers—an Internet link is a license to goof off.

As Robert Kraut and Vicki Lundmark's study reveals, email ₄₂ enhances distant communications while degrading local interactions. It perniciously gives us the illusion of making friends with faraway strangers while taking our attention away from our friends, family, and neighbors.

In the past, people in trouble relied on close, nearby friends for 43 support. Today, plenty of people turn to online support groups or chat rooms. Professor Mary Baker of Stanford reports that while she was expecting, she exchanged five email messages a day with a friend across the country . . . a woman she'd never met. Yet email pen pals can hardly provide the social support of a nearby friend or family member—if Professor Baker had to rush to the hospital, she could hardly get a ride from her email friend.

Today, it's natural enough to look to the Internet for a commu- 44 nity, since our real neighborhoods have been relentlessly undercut by television, automobiles, and urban renewal. Yet as more and more people turn to the Internet, our real communities receive even less human investment.

For the effect of instant electronic communications is to isolate us 45 from our colleagues next door. I met two computer jocks at a television station who spent their free time playing an Internet game with each other. Even though they sat five feet from each other, they'd communicate via email and rarely so much as glanced at each other.

Professor Zimbardo tells me that sometimes he sticks his head 46 into the office of a friend down the hall, with nothing more important than to say, "Hi!" "On several occasions, my greeting has been received with the shock of 'What's so important that you're invading my personal space? Why are you interrupting my productivity?' "

The price of computing at home—as in school and at work—is 47 far more than the cost of the hardware. The opportunity cost is our time, and it is taken out of our individual lives and our very real neighborhoods. The time you spend behind the monitor could be spent facing another person across a table or across a tennis court. Disguised as efficiency machines, digital time bandits steal our lives and undermine our communities.

Text as Mask: Gender, Play, and Performance on the Internet[1]

Brenda Danet

Part I: Gender, Mask, and Masquerade in Virtual Culture

It is a remarkable fact that many people who have never before been interested in cross-dressing as a member of the opposite gender are experimenting with gender identity in typed encounters on the Internet. Males are masquerading as females, and females are masquerading as males.[2] In cyberspace, *the typed text provides the mask.* Motivations for doing so are varied. Men are curious about what it is like to be a woman or seek the attention that female-presenting individuals typically receive. Women want to avoid being harassed sexually or to feel free to be more assertive. For still others, women and men, textual masquerade may be a source of titillation or a way to experiment with their sexuality.

The experimentation discussed in this chapter is just one of the new forms of virtual culture now developing in cyberspace. Virtual culture is a "culture of simulation" (Baudrillard, 1983; Jameson, 1984; Poster, 1990; Turkle, 1995, p. 10), of images with no necessary physical reality behind them, and of copies without originals (Baudrillard, 1983; Benjamin, 1969; Pinchbeck, 1994). Sherry Turkle suggested that it "is affecting our ideas about mind, body, self, and machine" (p. 10). It is also changing our ideas about social relations, conviviality and the forms of human communication we will consider "real," and "meaningful" in the 21st century.

[1] Earlier versions of this chapter were presented at a conference on "Masquerade and Gendered Identity," Venice, February 21–24, 1996 and at a conference in honor of Elihu Katz's 70th birthday, at the Van Leer Institute and Institute for Democracy, Jerusalem, May, 1996. Special thanks to Lee-Ellen Marvin and Keith Wilson for material on gender options on MediaMOO and LambdaMOO. Amia Lieblich led me to the "Baby X" study. Thanks to Pavel Curtis, Roger Crew, and other subscribers to MOO-Cows@xerox.com for information on gender options on MOOs. Discussions with Barbara Kirshenblatt-Gimblett and Lori Kendall have greatly benefited this chapter. Tsameret Wachenhauser provided technical help. For another treatment of themes of this chapter, discovered only after it was first drafted, see Dickel (1995).
[2] The growing literature on this topic includes Curtis (1996); Dickel (1995); Kendall (1996, in press); McRae (1996, 1997); Reid (1991, 1995, 1996); Stone (1991, 1996: chap. 3); Turkle (1995); van Gelder (1986).

Some people are leading double or multiple lives in cyberspace, 3 even with different gender identities. Others are trying out what it might mean to be gender-free, neither male nor female. Like Sherry Turkle (1995) and M. H. Dickel (1995), I believe that masquerading in this fashion promotes consciousness-raising about gender issues and might contribute to the long-term destabilization of the way we currently construct gender.

This chapter develops a research agenda for studies of textual 4 masquerade—the performance of gender, textual cross-dressing, and gender-neutrality—in synchronous chat modes. These topics are of interest to students of gender, cross-dressing, and transgenderism (e.g., Bem, 1993; Bornstein, 1994; Bullough & Bullough, 1993; Butler, 1990; Ekins & King, 1996; Garber, 1992; Herdt, 1994; Kessler & McKenna, 1978; Senft & Hom, 1996; Tseelon, 1995), masquerade and carnival (e.g., Bakhtin, 1984; Burke, 1978; Castle, 1986; Craft-Child, 1993; Docker, 1994; Part III; Turner, 1982), and the new virtual culture (e.g., Danet, Wachenhauser, Bechar-Israeli, Cividalli, & Rosenbaum-Tamari, 1995; Dickel, 1995; Jones, 1997; Porter, 1997; Stone, 1996; Turkle, 1995).

Writing, Play, and Performance in Synchronous Chat Modes

Experimentation with the performance of gender is just one of a 5 number of forms of playful expressivity in cyberspace, a domain in which many activities, of hackers, young people, and grown-ups, are subversive or even carnivalesque (Barlow, 1996; Danet, Ruedenberg, & Rosenbaum-Tamari 1997; Danet, Wachenhauser et al., 1995; Meyer & Thomas, 1990; Ruedenberg, Danet, & Rosenbaum-Tamari, 1995; Stone, 1996). In cyberspace it is always "night." Because communication is mainly text-based, people cannot see one another. Even basic characteristics such as age and gender are invisible. The anonymity and dynamic, playful quality of the medium have a powerful, disinhibiting effect on behavior. People allow themselves to behave in ways very different from ordinary everyday life, to express previously unexplored aspects of their personalities, much as they do when wearing masks and costumes at a carnival or a masked ball.

Synchronous chat modes (e.g., IRC [Internet Relay Chat], MUDs) 6 challenge our past assumptions about community, conviviality, and communication. Research is demonstrating that artful, stylized improvisation and wordplay flourish not only in face-to-face encounters but also among persons communicating remotely via computers (Danet, in press; Danet, Ruedenberg et al., 1997; Danet,

Wachenhauser et al., 1995; Kendall, 1996; Marvin, 1995; Ruedenberg et al., 1995; Werry 1996). Experiences in typed on-line chat can be powerfully "real," whether very exciting or very upsetting, despite the invisibility of the bodies of players (Dibbell, 1996; Ito, 1997; Jacobson, 1996; McRae, 1996, 1997; Turkle, 1995).

Part II: The Tyranny of Gender in the Real World

In this chapter, I adopt Erving Goffman's definition of gender: 7 "the culturally established correlates of sex" (Goffman, 1979, p. 1, cited in Ekins & King, 1996, p. 1). "We make a gender *attribution . . .* every time we see a new person" (Kessler & McKenna, 1978, p. 2). Our decision is based not on inspection of the sexual organs of individuals but on judgments about their performance in relation to culturally constructed gender categories. From early childhood, individuals learn to signal their gender identity in accord with gender stereotypes. They learn to *perform* "maleness" or "femaleness," "masculinity" or "femininity." So salient have gender and the perception of gender been to our consciousness that we may speak of *the tyranny of gender.* In modern Western culture we have been prisoners of an all-pervasive, two-category system. Thus, physicians "correct" children born with ambiguous sexual organs to fit one or the other of the two reigning categories (Bullough & Bullough, 1993, chap. 9; Ekins & King, 1996, Part III; Kessler, 1990).

The obsession with just two sexes and two genders is not uni- 8 versal. There is strong historical and anthropological evidence that some societies recognize a third and perhaps even a fourth gender (Ekins & King, 1996; Herdt, 1994; Kessler & McKenna, 1978, chap. 2; Ramet, 1996; Wikan, 1982), for example, the *hijra* in India (Jaffrey, 1996; Nanda, 1994).

The idea of a third (and perhaps even a fourth) gender is also rel- 9 evant for our own times. Whether or not one chooses to view gay men and lesbian women as third and fourth genders, perhaps transsexuals should be viewed as such (Bornstein, 1994; Connell 1987, p. 6, cited in Ekins & King, 1996, p. 2; Senft & Davis, 1996; Whittle, 1996).

The Pervasiveness of Gender Stereotypes

The pervasiveness of gender stereotypes in contemporary life is 10 easily documented. In one study, adults interacted with a 3-month-old infant in a yellow jumpsuit. When the infant was labeled a "girl," subjects chose a doll for it, rather than a football or teething ring (Seavey, Katz, & Zalk, 1975). By age one, children were shown pictures of adults of both genders and asked "Where is Mummy?" and "Where is Daddy?" already choose a picture of the "correct" gender (Belotti, 1976, p. 51). In another study, people were asked to describe the person who had sold them subway tokens. Gender was the first or second characteristic mentioned 100% of the time (Beall, 1993, p. 135, cited in Unger & Crawford, 1992).

Gender, Gender Ambiguity, and Fashion

Many prominent components of 20th-century fashion, for example, jeans, T-shirts, short hair cuts, and the preference for a slim, boyish figure for women, and longer hairstyles and earrings for men, have promoted an androgynous look. Think of Michael Jackson—with his light skin color, makeup, long hair, and costumes, he is neither black nor white, neither male nor female. At the same time, heterosexual individuals of both biological sexes, if not homosexual ones, rarely wish to be perceived as truly neither male nor female, as unequivocally neuter. Notwithstanding fashion's frequent encouragement of women to borrow items and modes of men's dress, "[i]t is characteristic for cross-gender clothing signals . . . to be accompanied by some symbolic qualification, contradiction, jibe, irony, exaggeration, etc., that advises the viewer not to take the cross-gender representation at face value" (Davis, 1992, p. 42). [11]

Thus, in a photograph of Marlene Dietrich wearing a man's suit, shirt, tie, and beret, other features besides her face give her away as a woman: her makeup, hourglass figure and protruding breasts (Lurie, 1981, p. 244). In Davis's (1992, p. 42) own example, a woman wearing otherwise "male" clothing softens her look with a scarf headband. Women trying to "dress for success" in business are told to wear suits but to add secondary "feminine" details (Davis, 1992; Molloy, 1977). [12]

As Goffman (1976) showed, advertisements encode gender in a host of subtle ways, constantly reinforcing our internalization of these cultural categories. This may be changing in the postmodern period. Some advertisements, for example, those of Calvin Klein, have been promoting a more genuinely androgynous look. On the face of it, the unisex look seems to be evidence of a softening of gender boundaries. This look peaked in the 1960s and 1970s. [13]

Nonetheless, although unisex fashion continues to be popular, by the late 1970s male fashion had returned to a more masculine look. Unisex is today primarily an option for women, thereby reinforcing inequality (Gottdeiner, 1992).

Gender and Gender Ambiguity in Film

Film after film plays on our curiosity about others' gender. In [14] *Victor/Victoria*, a woman, played by Julie Andrews, plays a man impersonating a woman; the audience knows of the impersonation and is invited to ask, "Does she really look like a man?" In *M. Butterfly* a man impersonates a woman, "taking in" both the audience and the person's lover—the high point of the play is the astonishing revelation that the "man" is "really" a woman. The play was based on the true story of a Chinese opera dancer and spy who had an affair with a French diplomat in the 1920s (Bullough & Bullough, 1993, p. 243; Garber, 1992, chap. 10). There is a similar shock effect in *The Crying Game*—the character Dil is a female-presenting person, an attractive "female" who happens to have a penis. The film confronts us with the fact that Dil herself is not bothered by her "condition," which conventional society cannot tolerate (van Lenning & Maas, 1996).

When male actors play women, as in *Some Like It Hot*, *Tootsie*, and [15] *Mrs. Doubtfire*, we scrutinize them to see how well they carry off their role. As in the case of *Victor/Victoria*, these films are less challenging to the social order than *The Crying Game*, because we never have any doubt as to the ascribed biological classification or sexual orientation of the "real" character, the real actor, or both (van Lenning & Maas, 1996).

Transsexuals and the Social Construction of Gender

Real-world (RL) transsexuals—who have undergone sex-change [16] operations—are a source of endless fascination. Do former males "really" now look female, or do they still look male? Thus, the photographs in Kate Bornstein's book on her transformation from a married, biological male to a transsexual lesbian invites readers to ask: Can that dashing male marine officer really be the same person as the attractive woman with the long, luxuriant hair, plunging neckline, and earrings? The cover of the autobiography of Mark Rees (1996), a female-to-male transsexual, teases us too, displaying both a photograph of a young person, ambiguously either a boy or girl, and the obviously masculine adult Rees, with a light mustache and beard. Autobiographical accounts of transsexuals document that hormonal intervention and surgical changes alone are not enough. These individuals work very hard to learn to perform their desired gender.[3]

Gender Ambiguity and Cross-Dressing as an Art Form

There *are* certain exceptions to the usual distaste for gender ambiguity and cross-dressing, notably, in contexts having to do with art, theater, and performance. The traditional theaters of both China and Japan cultivated the arts of the female impersonator (Garber, 1992, p. 245; Scott, 1966, p. 181). In traditional Japanese theater—*Kabuki*—actors specializing in *onnagata* (female impersonator) roles were cherished as artists who exquisitely mime femininity (Inoura & Kawatake, 1981, p. 142). To this day, *onnagata* actors are still the most famous stars of Kabuki (Inoura & Kawatake, 1981, p. 189). In the past they wore feminine dress offstage as well as on; today they live as men (Scott, 1966, p. 173). As for Western tradition, the film *Farinelli, il Castrato* reminds us that in Baroque opera, *castrati*, including Farinelli himself, were objects of worship like rock stars today. Castration at the age of 12 preserved the pure tone of the boy soprano. At first castrati sang mainly male roles but increasingly appeared in female roles; some lived as men, others as women (Garber, 1992, p. 254). The real Farinelli had an astonishing range, from middle baritone to very high Soprano (Hirshfeld, 1996a) and was able to perform vocal feats beyond the reach of conventional female or male singers (Hirshfeld, 1996b). 17

Another recent film that presents the idea of a third gender in the context of performance is *Priscilla, Queen of the Desert*, a vibrant, hilarious celebration of the *joie de vivre* and performing skills of three itinerant drag performers. At the same time, we learn of the sadness in these men-women's lives because they don't fit conventional gender categories. 18

Part III: Gender Games in Cyberspace

Until the advent of the digital era, the idea of a gender-free existence was conceivable only in science fiction. Feminist science fiction 19

---

[3] Resources for transsexuals learning to pass are available on the World Wide Web. See URL http://www.pond/com/~julie/general/gperlO.html (*A Cross-Dresser's Guide to Stepping Out*), and URL http://julie.pond.com,~julie (*The Gender Home Page*).

writers have experimented with this possibility. Ursula Le Guin's (1969) novel *The Left Hand of Darkness* is a "thought experiment" about the possibility of genuine cultural, as well as biological androgyny. In his "field notes," an observer of this imaginary society who came from Earth wrote,

> Our entire pattern of socio sexual interaction is non-existent here. The Gethenians do not see one another as men or women. This is almost impossible for our imaginations to accept. After all, what is the first question we ask about a newborn baby? Yet you cannot think of a Gethenian as an "it." They are not neuters. They are potentials . . . One is respected and judged only as human being. (pp. 94–95)

In this society, Bassnett (1991) noted,   20

> People exist in a state of non-gender until they come into "kemmer" when they develop sexually for a brief period randomly as either males or females, and consequently the absence of sexuality is a "continuous social factor" for most of the time. (p. 56)[4]

The Possibilities for Playing With Gender in Cyberspace

As I pointed out earlier, in text-based, digital communication,   21 conventional signals of gender, such as intonation and voice pitch, facial features, body image, nonverbal cues, dress, and demeanor, are absent. Thus, the idea of gender-free communication becomes conceivable for the first time. A well-known New Yorker cartoon brought this point home: Its caption is "On the Internet no one knows you're a dog."

Play with gender and with identity flourishes in chat modes, in   22 the *nom de plume* that players adopt and in their contributions. Individuals' real names may not be known. Until recently, at least, most of the participants on IRC and MUDs were young people, typically students, and more often than not, male. Players play with language, the software, cultural content of all kinds, as well as with aspects of their identity (Bechar-Israeli, 1995; Danet, 1995; Danet, Ruedenberg, et al., 1997; Danet, Wachenhauser, et al., 1995; Marvin, 1995; Ruedenberg, et al., 1995; Stivale, 1997; Turkle, 1995). Because

---

[4] Radical though her thought experiment was, Le Guin was attacked for not being radical enough. See Bassnett (1991, p. 56) and Le Guin (1989).

people can type in their pajamas in the middle of the night, it is easy for them to pretend to be someone else. According to Turkle (1995),

> You can be whoever you want to be. You can completely redefine yourself if you want. You can be the opposite sex. You can be more talkative. You can be less talkative . . . you can just be whoever you want, really. . . . You don't have to worry about the slots other people put you in as much. It's easier to change the way people perceive you, because all they've got is what you show them. They don't look at your body and make assumptions. They don't hear your accent and make assumptions. All they see are your words. (p. 184)

Although there are social and cultural constraints on individuals'   23 behavior, for women in particular, this medium is potentially very liberating. Not only is appearance neutralized, but the software generally guarantees to those who type that they will be "heard" without ha having to compete for the floor. At the same time, a growing literature claims that the subordinate status of women is being reproduced in cyberspace (Dickel, 1995; Hall, 1996; Herring, 1993, 1994b; Kramarae, 1995; Schmeiser, 1996; Wu, 1993). There is only an apparent contradiction here: Synchronous chat modes may offer possibilities for undermining the social arrangements and perceptions that asynchronous modes—discussion lists and newsgroups—merely reproduce.

Playing With Gender on IRC

On IRC many people are "regulars" in one or more channels.   24 Most people adopt a "nick," or nickname. To create a nick, one types, for example, "/nick topsy," and hits the enter key. Immediately, one's nick is registered for all to see as "topsy." Although players can change their nick at any moment, they generally choose one nick carefully and use it continuously. Players respect each others' rights over their nicks (Bechar-Israeli, 1995). Like RL masks, nicks (as well as personas on MUDs) echo the two great principles in nature: the *principle of camouflage* and the *principle of conspicuous marking* (Gombrich, 1984, p. 6). They both hide players' RL identity and call attention to the players in their virtual guise.

Reexamining a corpus of 260 nicks gathered from four IRC chan-   25 nels (Bechar-Israeli, 1995), I find that *less than one-fifth* invite an inference with respect to gender. Thus, <Arafat>, <dutchman>, and <madman> are all obviously male, either by cultural association (<Arafat>) or they are explicitly marked as male (the others ending in

Figure 1   The Players at a Virtual Party on IRC

Nick	Userid and Address	Additional Material
\<Lucia\>	soulr@vm1.huji.ac.il	
\<Thunder\>	root@xxxxxxxxxxxxxxxxx	(-: Raam/Chundeung :-)
\<Kang\>	GENGHISCON@xxxxxxx	(\<Drax the D\>)
\<Rikitiki\>	rpa3@xxxxxxxxxxxxxxxxx	
\<BlueAdept\>	dlahti@xxxxxxxxxxxxxx	
\<Jah\>	miksma3@xxxxxxxxxx	(Baba)
\<Lizardo\>	lizardo@xxxxxxxxxxxx	(Doctor Lizardo)
\<Teevie\>	ssac@xxxxxxxxxxxxxx	

*SOURCE: Reproduced from Danet, Ruedeberg, and Tamari, 1997.

-man) Similarly, *\<Sylvie\>*, *\<pcWoman\>*, and *\<Darkgirl\>* are female *\<Emigrant\>*, *\<meat\>* and *\<surfer\>*, on the other hand, are gender-neutral. There is no reliable way to find out whether the ostensible gender matches the RL one.

In a study of a virtual party on IRC in which the participants simulated "smoking dope" with typographic symbols, most of the nicks were unidentifiable with respect to gender (see Figure 1). Using her real name as her nick—*\<Lucia\>*—Lucia Ruedenberg, my collaborator, was the only obviously gendered player. One player used the nick *\<Kang\>*—the name of a male character in *Star Trek*. From extended interaction with \<Thunder\>, the main player in this sequence, both on-line and off, we knew that he was male (Danet, Ruedenberg, et al., 1997; Ruedenberg et al., 1995).

These findings suggest that IRC players can successfully camouflage their gender identity, even over long periods of time. Of course, many players with gender-ambiguous nicks may later reveal their gender. Thus, a person nicknamed *\<MeatLoaf\>* might flirt with players having clearly female nicks, inviting the inference that this person is male.

It is interesting to compare these results with Susan Kalcik's (1985) study of the "handles" chosen by female CB radio activists. In Kalcik's corpus, most women chose conventional female-marked handles, such as "*Sweet Sue*," "*Cinderella*," or "*Queen Bee*." Some women whose husbands were also involved in CB chose a handle reflecting their relationship to them, for example, "*North Star's Lady*," or "*Comanche's Angel*." By and large, women chose handles reflecting the two classic female stereotypes, the sex kitten (e.g., "*Hot Pants*," "*Bouncing Boobs*"), and the sweet, gentle woman ("*Sweet Pea*," "*Sugar Cookie*," "*Sweet Angel*"). Whereas some gender-neutral handles were chosen (e.g., *"Bookworm," "Stargazer"*), and there are even a few instances of male-sounding ones (*"Lucky Louie," "Samurai"*), these women did not play much with gender in the ways discussed in this chapter.

Playing With Gender on MUDs

Play with gender is much more elaborate and probably much 29 more far-reaching in its consequences on MUDs than on IRS. The first, and most famous, social MUD, LambdaMOO, was created by Pavel Curtis and others in 1990 (Curtis, 1996),[5] and now has about 8,000 characters; it has become the virtual equivalent of a small town (Coe, 1995). MediaMOO was created by Amy Bruckman while a doctoral student at MIT, for researchers of new media. Despite its professional goals, it is also very social, running a *"happy hour"* at the end of the work week. On LambdaMOO, the RL identity of the players behind the characters is not revealed, whereas on MediaMOO, in keeping with its partially professional nature, the RL names of players are known.[6] Thus, players are freer on LambdaMOO to experiment with role playing.

When they join a MUD, individuals create an elaborate "per- 30 sona" or "character," whose description can be read by anyone logged on to it (Bruckman, 1992, 1996; Turkle, 1995). Whereas IRC does not explicitly require players to attend to the matter of gender, MUDs do so.[7] After registering their character, players role play in this guise for months if not years. Thus, a male college student might create "Samantha, a gorgeous blonde with a fabulous figure," who conducts love affairs with males, has virtual sex, and even "gets married"—all on-line. Players may even play different fantasy characters, of different genders, in different MUDs *simultaneously*. Turkle tells of a male player who played four different characters in three different MUDs, including a seductive woman, a macho cowboy type, and a rabbit of unspecified gender. He told Turkle that reality "is just one more window" (Turkle, 1995, p. 13). The following account (Leslie, 1993) ilustrates aspects of the impersonation of females by males on MUDs:

---

[5] Roger Crew supplied the information about the year in which LambdaMOO was created.

[6] Personal electronic communication from Lee-Ellen Marvin. In MUDs, such as "BlueSky," in which many participants also know each other in real life, Kendall (1996, in press) reports that despite the use of on-line personas, there is relatively little role playing or cross-dressing.

[7] Benny Shanon called the importance of this difference to my attention.

Christian Sykes is no nerd: he's 23, married, a religious studies major at the University of Kansas... he decided to find out whether he could portray a woman convincingly. Many males who impersonate females on MUDs are easy to detect, for they behave not as real women do but rather as late-adolescent males wish they would, responding with enthusiasm to all sexual advances, sometimes in quite explicit terms; ... he kept the description of his character simple and as consistent with his own appearance as possible. Women on the MUD spoke among themselves about boyfriends, menstruation, or even gynecological problems, he drew upon lore gleaned from his wife and female friends.

Sykes' major revelation... was the extent of sexual harassment of women. Though not one person suspected Sykes' prank, he abandoned it after four months because he could not write programs without being constantly interrupted by male advances. Revealing the hoax didn't even end Sykes' problems, for one male player who apparently had a crush on Eris [his character's name] became so irate that he tried to get Sykes banished from the MUD.

The software of MUDs offers an amazing variety of genders. 31 Figure 2 lists the genders available on MediaMOO and LambdaMOO. Besides "male" and "female" one can choose "*neuter,*" "*either,*" "*spivak,*" "*splat,*" "*plural,*" "*egotistical,*" "*royal*" (as in the royal "we"), "2nd," and "person." Each gender has its own set of pronouns. Some are familiar from ordinary usage—for "neuter," the pronouns are "it, its, itself." In the case of "either," the player will be represented consistently with "s/he, him/her, his/her, his/hers/(him/her)self," and so on. To make the unfamiliar ones comprehensible, I have added permutations of the simple sentence "I read my book myself," in each of the genders. Thus, in the "royal we" choice, the sentence becomes "We are reading our book" (Figure 2).

MediaMOO recently added an additional choice not available on 32 LambdaMOO: "person." Players can say "Per reads per book perself." Such seemingly bizarre sentences are comprehensible when we recall that on MUDs action is rendered in the third person: chatting resembles writing collective fiction more than dramatic dialogue.

Origins of Gender Options

To learn the origins of these gender options, I contacted Pavel 33 Curtis, the main developer of LambdaMOO. Curtis referred me to Roger Crew, who had personally added the category "spivak" to the program in May, 1991:

Figure 2 Available Genders on MediaMOO and LambdaMOO

>> @gender male	Gender set to male.
Your pronouns:	he, him, his, his, himself, He, Him, His, His, Himself
Example:	He reads his book himself.
>> @gender female	Gender set to female.
Your pronouns:	she, her, her, hers, herself, She, Her, Her, Hers, Herself
Example:	She reads her book herself.
>> @gender neuter	Gender set to neuter.
Your pronouns:	it, it, its, its, itself, It, It, Its, Its, Itself
Example:	It reads its book itself.
>> @gender either	Gender set to either.
Your pronouns:	s/he, him/her, his/her, his/hers, (him/her)self, S/He, Him/Her, His/Her, His/Hers, (Him/Her)self
Example:	S/he reads his/her book him/herself.
>> @gender spivak	Gender set to Spivak.
Your pronouns:	e, em, eir, eirs, eirself, E, Em, Eir, Eirs, Eirself
Example:	E reads eir book eirself.
>> @gender splat	Gender set to splat.
Your pronouns:	*e,h*,h*,h*s,h*self, *E, H*, H*, H*s, H*self
Example:	*e reads h*s book h*self.
>> @gender plural	Gender set to plural.
Your pronouns:	they, them, their, theirs, themselves, They, Them, Their, Theirs, Themselves
Example:	They read their book themselves.
>> @gender egotistical	Gender set to egotistical. [36]
Your pronouns:	I, me, my, mine, myself, I, Me, My, Mine, Myself
Example:	I read my book myself.
>> @gender royal	Gender set to royal.
Your pronouns:	we, us, our, ours, ourselves, We, Us, Our, Ours, Ourselves
Example:	We read our book ourselves.
@gender 2nd	Gender set to 2nd.
Your pronouns:	you, you, your, yours, yourself, You, You, Your, Yours, Yourself
Example:	You read your book yourself.
@gender set to person.	
Your pronouns:	per, per, per, pers, perself, Per, Per, Per, Pers, Perself [37]
Example:	Per reads per book perself.

---

*MediaMOO only

I wrote some code and then introduced several extra "genders" (pronoun sets) to test it out, including, as something of a joke, various gender-neutral "genders" and, as even more of a joke, sets of pronouns that were in fact plural and/or non-3rd-person, thus totally violating the actual grammatical notion of gender. Nevertheless, some of these caught on, including—much to my dismay, actually—the Spivak "gender."[8]

He had named the "Spivak gender" for Michael Spivak, a mathematics professor who used gender-neutral pronouns in his textbooks.[9] Crew never dreamed that "spivak" would catch on, attributing its success to its intensive use by several particularly active individuals. As he puts it, "In a milieu where people were routinely being brown Labradors, space aliens, and fractal dragons, alternative pronoun sets seemed pretty ordinary"[10] When making his choices, Crew was quite conscious of the public debate about English grammatical gender and the issue of sexism in language in the United States.

As for "per," evidently, the inspiration came from science fiction. In Marge Piercy's (1979) novel *Woman on the Edge of Time*, persons in 21st-century society use it as the sole third-person pronoun when referring to others, thus obscuring the gender of those persons.[11] Finally, I learned that "splat" is the vocalization of the asterisk * in mathematics and computing.[12]

Actual Gender Choices on LambdaMOO and MediaMOO

Data on the distribution of actual gender choices on LambdaMOO and MediaMOO[13] are fascinating: Many players on both MUDs are choosing unconventional genders. The relative proportions choosing each gender are remarkably similar in the two MUDs (upperhalf of Table 1). The single most common choice is "male," followed by "female," but the biggest surprise is the substantial proportion choosing a category other than these two. To sharpen the contrast between categories, I collapsed them into just three (lower half of Table 1). On both MUDs, about half the players

---

[8] Personal e-mail communication from Roger Crew, March 15, 1996.

[9] The "spivak" gender category first appeared in Spivak (1990; McRae, 1996, footnote 6).

[10] Personal communication from Roger Crew, March 16, 1996.

[11] See "The Gender-free Pronoun" FAQ at URL http://www.eecis.udel.edu/~chao/gfp/. Pavel Curtis referred me to this source.

[12] See the Cyberlore Central Website at URLhttp://pass.wayne.edu/~twk/compfolk.html#play, the information for "Pronunciation Guide."

[13] These data were supplied to me by Lee-Ellen Marvin and Keith Weston, known on MUDs as "Luna" and "Lemper," respectively. Such data are available directly from the software at these sites.

Table 1 Conventional and Unconventional Genders Actually Chosen on MediaMOO and LambdaMOO

Gender	MediaMOO*	LambdaMOO
male	495	3651
female	197	2069
neuter	280	1162
spivak	10	74
either	9	15
plural	7	26
royal	6	30
splat	5	17
egotistical	2	16
2nd	2	5
person	2	—
Total	1015	7065
Percentage male	48.8	51.7
Percentage female	19.4	29.2
Percentage unconventional	31.8	19.1
	100.0%	100.0%
	(1015)	(7065)

*Breakdown as of January 17, 1996.
**Breakdown as of February 9, 1996.

choose "male" gender, with the proportions choosing "female" and "unconventional" or "neuter" reversed on the two MUDs. *On MediaMOO nearly a third chose an unconventional gender; on LambdaMOO it drops to about a fifth.* My 1996 figures for LambdaMOO jibe with Lon Kendall's (1996, p. 217) 1994 figures: 25.5% were unconventional; 23% were female and 53% male, suggesting that the general pattern is consistent over time.[14]

Sherry Turkle (1995) cited data that on a Japanese MUD with 1.5 million users, there is a ratio of four RL men to one RL woman, whereas among characters registered, the ratio is only 3 to 1. She concluded that "a significant number of players, many tens of thousands

---

[14]Kendall cautions that many guest characters are listed as neuter because they haven't chosen their gender classification. Thus, a better question is: what is the distribution of "regulars" by chosen gender?

of them, are virtually cross-dressing" (p. 212). In short, this is not a rare phenomenon.

"Spivak" and Other Unconventional Pronoun Usage at a MUD Wedding

Although its use is still relatively rare, "spivak" appears to have 38 become a salient part of MUD culture, as is indicated by the following hilarious text from a virtual wedding (Jacobson, 1996):

> Dearly belagged, we are connected here today, to join this [bride and groom] in wholly mootrimony. If there be any character here, who has any reason why this [couple] should not be joined together, let h^{**} speak now, or forever hold h^{**} peace. Do you, [groom's name], take this moowoman, [bride's name], to be your moofully wedded significant other, to connect with and to send hug-verbs, in lag and in line-noise-less-conditions, from this CST Time forward, until character reaping do you part? . . . . Do you, [groom's name and bride's name] promise to love, cherish, and support each other, for paid phone-bills or unpaid, in gloom and in sunshine, for agreement or disagreement, from this moment unto forever, as long as the Internet shall last? . . . . [After receiving confirmatory answers, he intones] May the blessings of the Bovine Illuminati fall upon this couple. May the Internet guide and never disconnect on them. May the curse of line-noise never intrude upon their passionate emotings. May they always page each other with kind and loving words, and may their RL phone calls be as wonderful as their VR existence. . . . [Finally, he concludes the ceremony] *Ladies, Gentlemen, and Spivaks,* [italics added] under the authority of my position as Master of Ceremonies, I present to you, [names of groom and bride], Man, and wife, Woman, and husband. May they connect in harmony, forever!!! (p. 470)

Note also the use of h^{**} to blend "him" and "her," as provided by 39 the "splat" option (see Figure 2).[15]

Additional Evidence of Play With Gender

Besides the fixed gender options on MUDs, players also can cre- 40 ate their own idiosyncratic gender, though few players do so. Thus,

---

[15]For further discussion of the use of spivaks on MUDs, see McRae (1996, 1997).

on LambdaMOO, in addition to the 7,065 persons choosing a fixed gender category, another 243 persons, not shown in Table 1, created their own. On MediaMOO, in addition to the 1,015 choosing one of the fixed genders, another 40 tailored their own.

Choices jibe with the patterns already discussed. On both MUDs, 41 the large majority of nonstandard choices are clearly neutral, for example, "Chaos," "salty," "neutral," "opus," and "none" on MediaMOO, or "lover," "me," "Ghost," "wood," and "married" on LambdaMOO. Thus, the proportions choosing neutral genders are actually slightly higher than those shown in the lower half of Table 1. But surely the significance of these data lies not only in percentages. If we combine the numbers for MediaMOO and LambdaMOO, between 1,500 and 2,000 persons are playing a neutral character![16] Also worth noting are choices like "whatever I feel at the time" ("Tanya") or "mood-dependent, usually neuter" ("The-Prisoner") "s-he" ("Natalia") for three characters on LambdaMOO.

The majority of players on MUDs and in cyberspace generally 42 are known to be male. Until recently, a figure of 80% male and 20% female was widely quoted for persons active on the Internet; a recent survey indicates that the proportion of women is still low but now has risen to 30%.[17] Thus, we can be quite sure that many males on both MUDs are choosing either "female" or some unconventional gender. Unfortunately, data are not available on the match or lack of match between RL and MUD gender identity for LambdaMOO. In the case of MediaMOO, because RL names are known, in principle one might be able to figure out the actual gender of players from their first names—except, of course, in cases where the RL person has a gender-ambiguous name, such as Lee."

Textual Cross-Dressing and Getting Into Trouble

As the account from the Leslie (1993) article indicated, players 43 who cross-dress textually sometimes get into trouble (Stone, 1991, 1996, chap. 3; van Gelder, 1986). For instance, a New York Jewish male psychiatrist in his 50s played a female called "Talkin' Lady" on Compuserve; he created an elaborate persona of a woman who had been in a car accident in which her fiance had been killed. At first "depressed," "she" gradually became more outgoing and made

---

[16] A word of caution: some characters may be inactive; personal communication from Lee-Ellen Marvin.

[17] See URL http://www.cc.gatech.edu/gvu/user_surveys/survey-10-1995/#exec.

many friends. Eventually the subterfuge was discovered, much to the chagrin of those who had been taken in (van Gelder, 1986).[18]

A couple called "Mik" and "Sue" met and fell in love on MUD1. [44] For a very long stretch "Sue" was able to pass as a woman because she presented a coherent and consistent image. One person (Reid, 1994) who had interacted extensively with "Sue" reported,

> it had occurred to me several times that Sue might have been male, but every "test" I set was passed with flying colours. We'd even get little unsolicited details, like when she didn't reply to a message immediately because she'd just snagged a nail. It was little details like this which made her so convincing.[19]

Part IV: Questions for Research

In the final portion of this chapter, I propose a set of research [45] questions that integrate the study of gender experimentation on-line with literature on RL gender, language and gender, carnival and masquerade, and interactive writing as playful performance At least on the face of it, textual cross-dressing should be much easier than the RL variety. Nonetheless, it may be much more difficult than appears at first glance.

"Once [males] are on-line as female, they soon find that main- [46] taining this fiction is difficult. To pass as a woman for any length of time requires understanding how gender inflects speech, manner, the interpretation of experience" (Turkle, 1995, p. 212). Elizabeth Reid's (1994) experience while doing on-line ethnography for her MA thesis on MUDs confirms these difficulties:

> It is indeed a truly disorienting experience the first time one finds oneself being treated as a member of the opposite sex. My own forays into the realm of virtual masculinity were at first frightening experiences. Once deprived of the social tools which I, as female, was used to deploying and relying on, *I felt rudderless, unable to negotiate the most simple of social interactions. I did not know how to speak, whether to women or to "other" men, and I was thrown off balance by the ways in which other people spoke to me. It took much practice to learn to navigate these unfamiliar channels, an experience that*

---

[18]There are many versions of this story; for some variations, see Stone (1996, chap. 3) and Turkle (1995, pp. 228–230).

[19]The full text of this case is available in an earlier version of this chapter, at URL http://atar.mscc.huji.ac.il/~msdanet/mask.html, or in Reid's (1994) thesis. "Sue" turned out to be a man arrested for financial fraud in real life.

gave me a greater understanding of the mechanics of sexual politics than any other I have ever had [italics added]. (chap. 3)

I propose to problematize these linguistic and textual aspects of   47
masquerade and the performance of gender on-line. Here are some
questions for future investigation:

1. *What types of personae do players create? What are the cultural sources of these personae, for example, science fiction, fairy tales, myths? What types of personae are mapped onto the various gender choices offered by the software? In particular what personae are invented for gender-neutral characters?*

2. *What is the textual equivalent of visual éclat in RL masquerades?* Terry Castle (1986) has written of 18th-century English masquerades:

   The overriding object of costume, obviously, was to gratify, horrify, or seduce others. It was the masquerader's duty to be beautiful or uncanny, but never insipid. Several anti-conventions defined how such a visual éclat was to be achieved.

   The costume's object was radical festivity, a violent transformation of everyday appearance . . . one was obliged to appear . . . as one's opposite . . . masqueraders exploited a host of symbolic oppositions . . . sexual, economic, and racial incongruities; the oppositions between human and animal, natural and supernatural, past and present, the living and the dead. (pp. 75–76)

   How is éclat accomplished when the only resources at one's dis-   48
   posal are words?

3. *What are the similarities and differences between the games played at RL carnivals and masked balls and those on MUDs and in IRC channels? What RL carnival tradition or period, if any, is comparable and why? In particular, what is the significance of the reduced presence of the body in on-line masquerades, and how does this relate to the performance of gender, gender games and sexuality?* The evidence thus far suggests, paradoxically, that the atmosphere in on-line masquerades can be nearly as eroticized as in RL ones and in some cases perhaps even more so (McRae, 1996, 1997). To "wear text as mask" is potentially as much of a tease as to wear a "domino," the all-encompassing, neutering black cloak and mask worn by many men and women, in carnivals all over 18th-century Europe. As Castle (1986) pointed out,

Certainly, for those without the imagination or the exhibitionistic elan needed to wear more spectacular costume, the domino was a convenient choice. At the same time, its somewhat sinister power of effacement, its utter incommunicativeness, was in its own way compelling. What Caillois has written of the archtypal black mask, "the mask reduced to its essentials, elegant and abstract," also applies to the domino ... the quintessential sign of erotic and political cabal, the mark of intrigue itself. (p. 59)

One thing is clear: the preoccupation with class reversals so [49] characteristic of RL European carnivals over the centuries is absent; at present, on-line masqueraders are a relatively homogeneous elite of fairly affluent, educated, computer-literate individuals.

4. *How are gender and gender-bending performed?* What linguistic and substantive features characterize on-line performance? How are cross-dressing and gender-neutrality performed, in both substance and style? For ideas one could turn to the research literature on language, discourse and gender in the real world (Buckholz & Hall, 1995; Coates, 1986; Graddol & Swann, 1989; Herring, 1993; Lakoff, 1975; Philips, Steele, & Tanz, 1987; Smith, 1985; Tannen, 1990, 1993, 1994; Thorne & Henley, 1975), and on the Net (Cherny, 1994; Hall, 1996; Herring, 1993, 1994a, 1994b; Herring, Johnson, & DiBenedetto, 1995; Kendall, 1996, in press; McRae, 1996, 1997; Senft & Hom, 1996; Wu, 1993), feminist stylistics (Cameron, 1992; Mills, 1995), and the scripts of films in which men play women and vice versa. Because films originate as words—scripts—scriptwriters probably assign stereotypical, even caricatured female style to these characters.[20]

    In particular, what differences are there between the communication styles of genuine and pretend males and between genuine and pretend females? Do cross-dressed males caricature textual femininity, just as RL drag queens parody embodied femininity? Do people pretending to be gay men simulate a stereotype of gay speech? (Hall, 1996).

5. *What can the availability and use of gender-free pronouns on MUDs contribute to the debate about sexism in RL language?* This issue has a long history of debate (e.g., Baron, 1986; Cameron, 1992; MacKay, 1983; Martyna, 1980; Smith, 1985, chap. 3). Can extend-

---

[20]I am thinking for example, of "Mrs. Doubtfire's" habit of concluding utterances to her "employer" with "dear," as in "That's, a lovely blouse, dear."

ed use of neutral pronouns change perceptions about one's own and others' gender, for children, if not for adults? Roger Crew, of LambdaMOO, has suggested that, in addition to players being able to experiment with choice of gender themselves, one might also configure the computer program so as to make the gender of messages *received* optional. Thus, a person could choose to experience the virtual world as all-male, all-female, or all-neuter! Might this not also offer a mode of fostering gender-free perceptions in children—an hour or two every day in a fully gender-neutral environment, while they are still quite young?[21]

6. *When does textual cross-dressing succeed, and when does it breakdown and why?* The beginning of an answer to this question lies, apparently, in Goffman's (1974) concepts of coherence and consistency. Successful "passers" present a coherent, self-consistent image; but how is this constructed textually? Is "passing" mainly a matter of supplying consistent, coherent substantive cues, as the examples from Leslie (1993) and Reid (1994), suggest, or is it also a matter of packaging one's contributions linguistically in stereotypical ways?

7. *How is gender experimentation different on IRC and on MUDs?* Is experimentation more extensive and more profound in its consequences on MUDs (and therefore more interesting as a site for research), as I suspect?[22] Earlier, I suggested that in choosing to call oneself <meatloaf> or <pentium> on IRC, one is opting for a gender-neutral nick. It is also possible that individuals are playing primarily with *other* categories: with the animal or vegetable or mineral distinction, or with the animate or inanimate distinction, and not with gender.

8. *Why is there so much interest in gender-bending on the Net right now?* Is it merely an extension of the obsession with cross-dressing in contemporary (and past) culture generally (Garber, 1992), in films, and in a veritable flood of print publications, or are there other cultural forces at work too? Is it a temporary response to the novelty of new technology, or will it persist as cyberspace evolves? As more and more people develop person-

---

[21] Personal communication from Roger Crew, March 16, 1996. Of course, very young children do not know how to type, and if we wait till they *can* type, gender stereotypes already will be deeply entrenched.

[22] Kendall's (1996, in press) portrayal of interaction on "BlueSky" suggested that this MUD is more like IRC channels such as #*gb* ("Great Britain"), in which individuals have strong RL ties and do not engage in much role play. Clearly, one should avoid generalizing about all IRC channels versus all MUDs. There are also IRC channels with rich role playing and fantasy.

al Web sites and increasingly want to become known on the Internet, the potential for extended masquerade may decline, unless chat modes continue, to guarantee anonymity.

9. *What is the wider cultural significance of experimentation with gender on-line? Can it truly destabilize our current gender categories?* Will research strengthen Sherry Turkle's (1995) claim that in this postmodern era, identity has become a fluid, floating thing—where the "virtual" is as real as the "real," and where, multiple identities of differing genders can be maintained simultaneously, even over long periods of time?

Terry Castle (1986, p. 72 ff.) rightly argued that we must distinguish between individual experience, highlighted in Sherry Turkle's (1995) research, and a broader anthropological view. Some analysts of carnival argue that it offers only temporary respite from the tyranny of hierarchy and even reinforces it, whereas others see it as promoting genuine social and cultural change. Of course this would vary with the particular context and historical era. Castle (1986, pp. 90–91) distinguished between imitation of the powerless by the powerful (men impersonating women) and imitation of the powerful by the powerless (women impersonating men): downward impersonation is generally merely comic, vulgar, not really provocative. Because men currently dominate the design and use of technology in cyberspace, and because the numbers of individuals now engaging in textual masquerades are still fairly small, the prospects for genuine change seem very limited, at least until women become equal participants in cyberspace (Kramarae, 1995).

After a year of fieldwork on MUDs, Lori Kendall expressed considerable pessimism about the possibility of change; in the MUD she studied, whatever gender people chose for their characters, they often were pressed to reveal their RL gender (Kendall, 1996, pp. 217–218). Moreover, when attempting to role-play the opposite gender, players often resort to gender stereotypes, thereby, perhaps, actually reinforcing conventional gender thinking, rather than destabilizing it (Kendall, 1996; McRae, 1996, pp. 249–250). One thing is sure: these phenomena are much too new to generate facile generalizations. Every virtual environment is its own little world, with a unique subculture. Thus, what characterizes a fairly stable group of people interacting on one particular IRC channel or one MUD may not be characteristic of others.

10. *How will the advent of video conferencing alter these experiments with gender identity?* There is already much speculation about

whether video conferencing will replace textual communication in cyberspace. Technologies such as CU-SeeME can be used together with programs like IRC; more sophisticated video conferencing equipment is already in use among corporations. When full video possibilities become widespread, will the current spate of gender-bending disappear?

Perhaps not: Some argue that text will continue to be the preferred medium even when video is available, not only because it is cheaper but because its limited technical possibilities offer a creative challenge to users and because the anonymity of text will continue to have its charms. Another recent development offers additional resources for fantasy and experimentation. Software such as "The Palace" enables players to adopt an avatar—a graphic, virtual embodiment of their virtual selves that they can move around in a three-dimensional environment, "dress" and "accessorize." The image may be of a person, an object, or a living thing such as a butterfly. Individuals continue to type their words; thus the masking of identity is preserved.

If and when full video does arrive and becomes widely available, it will be harder to pass as a member of the opposite gender or to pretend to be gender-free than in the text-based virtual environments I have discussed in this chapter. On the other hand, video could offer marvelous new opportunities for dressing up!

References

Bahktin, M. (1984). *Rabelais and his world* (H. Iswolsky, Trans.). Bloomington: Indiana University Press.

Barlow, J. P. (1996). Crime and puzzlement. In P. Ludlow (Ed.), *High noon on the electronic frontier: Conceptual issues in cyberspace* (pp. 459–486). Cambridge: MIT Press.

Baron, D. (1986). *Grammar and gender*. New Haven, CT: Yale University Press.

Bassnett, S. (1991). Remaking the old world: Ursula Le Guin and the American tradition. In L. Armitt (Ed.), *Where no man has gone before: Women and science fiction* (pp. 50–66). New York: Routledge.

Baudrillard, J. (1983). *Simulations*. New York: Semiotext(e).

Bechar-Israeli, H. (1995). From <Bonehead> to <cLoNehEAd>: Nicknames, play and identity on Internet Relay Chat. In B. Danet (Ed.), *Play and performance in computer-mediated communication*

[Special issue]. *Journal of Computer-Mediated Communication, 1*(2). Available: URL http://jcmc.huji.ac.il/vol1/issue2/ or URL http://www.usc.edu/dept/annenberg/vol1/issue2/.

Belotti, E. G. (1976). *What are little girls made of? The roots of feminine stereotypes.* New York: Schocken.

Bern, S. L. (1993). *The lenses of gender: Transforming the debate on sexual inequality.* New Haven, CT: Yale University Press.

Benjamin, W. (1969). The work of art in the age of mechanical reproduction (H. Zohn, Trans.). In H. Arendt (Ed.), *Illuminations* (pp. 219–253). New York: Schocken.

Bornstein, K. (1994). *Gender outlaw: On men, women, and the rest of us.* New York: Routledge.

Bruckman, A. (1992). *Identity-workshop: Emergent social and psychological phenomena in text-based virtual reality.* Available: URL http://www.cc.gatech.edu/fac/Amy.Bruckman/papers/index.html

Bruckman, A. (1996). Gender swapping on the Internet. In P. Ludlow (Ed.), *High noon on the electronic frontier: Conceptual issues in cyberspace* (pp. 317–325). Cambridge: MIT Press. Also available: URL http://www.cc.gatech.edu/fac/Amy.Bruckman/papers/index.html

Bucholz, M., & Hall, K. (Eds.). (1995) *Gender articulated: Language and the socially constructed self.* New York: Routledge.

Bullough, V. L., & Bullough, B. (1993). *Cross dressing, sex, and gender.* Philadelphia: University of Pennsylvania Press.

Burke, P. (1978). *Popular culture in early modern Europe.* London: Temple Smith.

Butler, J. P. (1990). *Gender trouble: Feminism and the subversion of identity.* New York: Routledge.

Cameron, D. (1992). *Feminism and linguistic theory.* New York: Macmillan.

Castle, T. (1986). *Masquerade and civilization: The carnivalesque in 18th-century English culture and fiction.* Stanford, CA: Stanford University Press.

Cherny, L. (1994, April). Gender differences in text-based virtual reality. *Proceedings of the Berkeley conference on women and language.* Available: URL http://bhasha.stanford.edu/~cherny/genderMOO.html

Coates, J. (1986). *Women, men, and language.* New York: Longman.

Coe, C. (1995, November). *Difference and utopia in an electronic community.* Paper presented at the Annual Meeting of the American Anthropological Association, Washington, DC.

Connell, R. W. (1987). *Gender and power*. Oxford, UK: Basil Blackwell.

Craft-Child, C. (1993). *Masquerade and gender: Disguise and female identity in 18th century fiction by women*. University Park: Pennsylvania State University Press.

Curtis, P. (1996). MUDding: Social phenomena in text-based virtual realities. In P. Ludlow, (Ed.), *High noon on the electronic frontier: Conceptual issues in cyberspace* (pp. 347–374). Cambridge: MIT Press.

Danet, B. (Ed.). (1995). *Play and performance in computer-mediated communication* [Special issue]. *Journal of Computer-Mediated Communication, 1*(2). Available: URL http://jcmc.huji.ac.il/vol1/issue2/ or URL http://www.asc.edu/dept/annenberg/vol1/issue2/

Danet, B. (in press). *Keybo@rd K@perz: Studies of digital communication*.

Danet, B., Ruedenberg, L., & Rosenbaum-Tamari, Y. (1997). 'Hmmm . . . where's that smoke coming from?' Writing, play and performance on Internet Relay Chat. In F. Sudweeks, M. McLaughlin, & S. Rafaeli (Eds.), Network and netplay: Virtual groups on the Internet [Special issue]. *Journal of Computer-Mediated Communication, 4*(2). Available: URL http://jcmc.huji.ac.il/vol2/issue4/ or URL http://www.usc.edu/dept/annenberg/vol2/issue4/. Abridged version. Full version in book of same title, Cambridge, MA: AAAI/MIT Press, 1998, pp. 41–76.

Danet, B., Wachenhauser, T., Bechar-Israeli, T., Cividalli, A., & Rosenbaum-Tamari, Y. (1995). Curtain time 20:00 GMT: Experiments in virtual theater on Internet Relay Chat. In B. Danet (Ed.), *Play and performance in computer-mediated communication* [Special issue]. *Journal of Computer-Mediated Communication, 1*(2). Available: URL http://jcmc.huji.ac.il/vol1/issue2/ or URL http://www.usc.edu/dept/annenberg/vol1/issue2/

Davis, F. (1992). *Fashion, culture, and identity*. Chicago: University of Chicago Press.

Dibbell, J. (1996). A rape in cyberspace; or how an evil clown, a Haitian trickster spirit, two wizards, and a cast of dozens turned a database into a society. In P. Ludlow (Ed.), *High noon on the electronic frontier: Conceptual issues in cyberspace* (pp. 375–396). Cambridge: MIT Press.

Dickel, M. H. (1995). Bent gender: Virtual disruptions of gender and sexual identity. In S. Doheny-Farina (Ed.), *Networked virtual realities* [Special issue]. *EJC: Electronic Journal of Communication, 5*(4). Available to members from Comserve at URL http://www.cios.org.

Docker, J. (1994). *Postmodernism and popular culture: A cultural history.* Cambridge, UK: Cambridge University Press.

Ekins, R., & King, D. (Eds.). (1996). *Blending genders: Social aspects of cross-dressing and sex-changing.* New York: Routledge.

Garber, M. (1992). *Vested interests: Cross-dressing and cultural anxiety.* New York: Penguin.

Goffman, E. (1974). *Frame analysis. An essay on the organization of experience.* Cambridge, MA: Harvard University Press.

Goffman, E. (1976). *Gender advertisements.* London: Macmillan.

Gombrich, E. H. (1984). *The sense of order: A study of the psychology of decorative art.* London: Phaidon.

Gottdeiner, M. (1992). Fashion and gender role change. In M. Gottdeiner (Ed.), *Postmodern semiotics: Material culture and the forms of post modern life* (pp. 209–232). Oxford, UK: Basil Blackwell.

Graddol, D., & Swann, J. (1989). *Gender voices.* Oxford, UK: Basil Blackwell.

Hall, K. (1996). Cyberfeminism. In S.C. Herring (Ed.), *Computer-mediated communication: Linguistic, social, and cross-cultural perspectives* (pp. 147–170). Philadelphia: John Benjamins.

Herdt, G. (Ed.). (1994). *Third sex, third gender: Beyond sexual dimorphism in culture and history.* New York: Zone Books.

Herring, S.C. (1993). Gender and democracy in computer-mediated communication. *EJC: Electronic Journal of Communication, 3* (2).Available to members from Comserve at URL http://www.cios.org.

Herring, S. C. (1994a, June). *Gender differences in computer-mediated communication: Bringing familiar baggage to the new frontier.* Keynote talk at panel, *Making the Net*Work*: Is there a Z39.50 in Gender Communication?* Paper presented at the annual meeting of the American Library Association, Miami, Florida.

Herring, S. C. (1994b). Politeness in computer culture: Why women thank and men flame. In M. Bucholtz, A. Liang, & L. Sutton (Eds.), *Communication in, through, and across cultures: Proceedings of the third Berkeley women and language conference.* Berkeley, CA: Berkeley Women and Language Group.

Herring, S. C., Johnson, D., & DiBenedetto, T. (1995). "This discussion is going too far!" Male resistance to female participation on the Internet. In M. Bucholtz & K. Hall (Eds.), *Gender articulated: Language and the socially constructed self.* New York: Routledge.

Hirshfeld, A. (1996a, April 5). He was more than a woman, he was a work of art: A meditation on castration, homosexuality, and harnessed voices. *Ha'aretz,* (Hebrew).

Hirshfeld, A. (1996b, April 12). The operatic voice is blood. *Ha'aretz*, (Hebrew).

Inoura, Y., & Kawatake, T. (1981). *The traditional theater of Japan*. New York: Weatherhill.

Ito, M. (1997). Virtually embodied: The reality of fantasy in a Multi-User Dungeon. In D. Porter (Ed.), *Internet culture* (pp. 87–110). New York: Routledge.

Jacobson, D. (1996). Contexts and cues in cyberspace: The pragmatics of naming in text-based virtual realities, *Journal of Anthropological Research, 52*, 461–479.

Jaffrey, Z. (1996). *The invisibles: A tale of the eunuchs of India*. New York: Pantheon

Jameson, F. (1984). Postmodernism, or the cultural logic of late capitalism. *New Left Review, 146*, 53–92.

Jones, S. G. (Ed.). (1997). *Virtual culture: Identity and communication in cybersociety*. London: Sage.

Kalcik, S. (1985). Women's handles and the performance of identity in the CB community. In R. Jordan & S. Kalcik (Eds.), *Women's folklore, women's culture*. Philadelphia: University of Pennsylvania Press.

Kendall, L. (1996). MUDder? I Hardly Know 'Er! Adventures of a Feminist MUDder. In L. Cherny & E. R. Weise (Eds.), *Wired_ women: Gender and new realities in cyberspace* (pp. 207–223). Seattle, WA: Seal Press.

Kendall, L. (in press). Meaning and identity in "cyberspace": The performance of gender, class, and race on-line. *Symbolic Interaction*.

Kessler, S. J. (1990). The medical construction of gender: Case management of intersexed infants, *Signs: Journal of Women in Culture & Society, 16*(1), 5–25.

Kessler, S. J., & McKenna, W. (1978). *Gender: An ethnomethodological approach*. New York: Wiley.

Kramarae, C. (1993). A backstage critique of virtual reality. In S. C. Jones (Ed.), *CyberSociety: Computer-mediated communication and community* (pp. 36–56). Thousand Oaks, CA: Sage.

Lakoff, R. (1975). *Language and Woman's place*. New York: Harper & Row.

Le Guin, U. K. (1969). *The left hand of darkness*. New York: Ace.

La Guin, U. K. (1989). Is gender necessary? In U. K. Le Guin (Ed.), *The language of the night*. London: Women's Press.

Leslie, J. (1993, Sept.). Technology: MUDroom. *Atlantic Monthly, 272*, 28–34. Also available as electronic ms. from Leslie at jacques@well.sf.ca.us.

Lurie, A. (1981). *The language of clothes*. New York: Vintage.

MacKay, D. G. (1983). Prescriptive grammar and the pronoun problem. In B. Thorne, C. Kramarae, & N. Henley (Eds.), *Language, gender, and society* (pp. 38–53). Rowley, MA: Newbury House.

Martyna, W. (1980). Beyond the he/man approach. *Signs: Journal of Women in Culture & Society, 5*, 131–138.

Marvin, L. (1995). Spoof, spam, lurk, and lag: Aesthetics of text-based virtual realities. In B. Danet (Ed.), *Play and performance in computer-mediated communication* [Special issue]. *Journal of Computer-Mediated Communication, 1*(2). Available: URL http://jcmc.huji.ac.il/vol1/issue2/ or URL http://www.asc.edu/dept/annenberg/vol1/issue2/

McRae, S. (1996). Coming apart at the seams: Sex, text and the virtual body. In L. Cherny & E. R. Weise (Eds.), *Wired_women: Gender and new realities in cyberspace* (pp. 242–264). Seattle, WA: Seal Press.

McRae, S. (1997). Flesh made word: Sex, text and the virtual body. In D. Porter (Ed.), *Internet culture* (pp. 73–86). New York: Routledge.

Meyer, G., & Thomas. J. (1990). The baudy world of the byte bandit A postmodernist interpretation of the computer underground. In F. Schmalleger (Ed.), *Computers in criminal justice* (pp. 31–67). Bristol, IN: Wyndham Hall. Also available: URL www.soci.niu.edu/~gmeyer/baudy.html

Mills, S. (1995). *Feminist stylistics*. New York: Routledge.

Molloy, J. (1977). *The woman's dress for success book*. New York: Warner.

Nanda, H. (1994). Hijras: An alternative sex and gender role in India. In G. Herdt (Ed.), *Third sex, third gender: Beyond sexual dimorphism in culture and history* (pp. 373–418). New York: Zone Books.

Philips, S. U., Steele, S., & Tanz, C. (Eds.). (1987). *Language, gender, and sex in comparative perspective*. Cambridge, UK: Cambridge University Press.

Piercy, M. (1979). *Woman on the edge of time*. London: The Women's Press.

Pinchbeck, D. (1994). State of the art. *Wired, 2*, 157–158, 206–208.

Porter, D. (Ed.). (1997). *Internet culture*. New York: Routledge.

Poster, M. (1990). *The mode of information: Poststructuralisms and contexts*. Chicago: University of Chicago Press.

Ramet, S. P. (Ed.). (1996). *Gender reversals & gender cultures*. New York: Routledge.

Rees, M. (1996). *Dear sir or madam: The autobiography of a female-to-male transsexual*. London: Cassell.

Reid, E. (1991). Electropolis: Communication and community on Internet Relay Chat. Available: URL http://members.xoom.

com/elizrs/ Excerpted as Communication and community on Internet Relay Chat Constructing communities (pp. 397–412). In P. Ludlow (Ed.), *High noon on the electronic frontier: Conceptual issues in cyberspace*, 1996, 397–412. Cambridge: MIT Press.

Reid, E. (1994). *Cultural formations in text-based virtual realities.* Unpublished Masters' thesis, University of Melbourne, Australia. Available: URL www.crl.com/~emr/cult-form.html

Reid, E. (1995). Virtual worlds: Culture and imagination. In S. G. Jones (Ed.), *CyberSociety: Computer-mediated communication and community* (pp. 164–183). Thousand Oaks, CA: Sage.

Reid, E. (1996). Text-based virtual realities: Identity and the cyborg body. In P. Ludlow (Ed.), *High noon on the electronic frontier: Conceptual issues in cyberspace* (pp. 327–345). Cambridge: MIT Press.

Rolfe, B. (1977). *Behind the mask.* Oakland, CA: Persona Books.

Ruedenberg, L., Danet, B., & Rosenbaum-Tamari, Y. (1995). Virtual virtuosos: Play and performance at the computer keyboard. *EJC: Electronic Journal of Communication, 5*(4). Available to members from Comserve at URL http://www.cios.org, or at URL http://atar.mscc.huji.ac.il/7Emsdanet/virt.htm

Schmeiser, L. (Ed.). (1996, March). Women and gender on-line [Special issue]. *Computer-Mediated Communication Magazine.* Available URL http://www.december.com/cmc/mag/1996/mar/ed.html

Scott, A. C. (1966). *The kabuki theatre of Japan.* New York: Macmillan.

Seavey, C. A., Katz, P. A., & Zalk, S. R. (1975). Baby X: The effects of gender labels on adult responses to infants. *Sex Roles, 9,* 103–110.

Senft, T. M., & Davis, K. (1996). Modem butterfly reconsidered. In T. M Senft & S. Horn (Eds.), *Sexuality and cyberspace: Performing the digital body* (pp. 69–104) [Special issue]. *Women and performance, 17*(1). Also available: URL http://www.echonyc.com/~women/Issuel7/senftmodem.html

Senft, T. M., & Horn, S. (Eds.) (1996). Sexuality and cyberspace: Performing the digital body [Special issue]. *Women and Performance, 17(1),* 69–104.

Shaw, D. F. (1997). Gay men and computer communication: A discourse of sex and identity in cyberspace. In S. G. Jones (Ed.), *Virtual culture: Identity and communication in cybersociety* (pp. 133–145). London: Sage.

Smith, P. M. (1985). *Language, the sexes and society*. Oxford, UK: Basil Blackwell.

Spivak, M. (1990). *The joy of TEX: A gourmet guide to typesetting with the AMS-TEX macro package*. Providence, RI: American Mathematical Society.

Stivale, C. J. (1997). Spam: Heteroglossia and Harassment in cyberspace. In D. Porter (Ed.), *Internet culture* (pp. 133–144). New York: Routledge.

Stone, A. R. (1991). Will the real body please stand up? Boundary stories about virtual cultures. In M. Benedikt (Ed.), *Cyberspace: First steps* (pp. 81–118). Cambridge: MIT Press.

Stone, A. R. (1996). *The war of desire and technology*. Cambridge: MIT Press.

Tannen, D. (1990). *You just don't understand: Women and men in conversation*. New York: Ballantine.

Tannen, D. (Ed.). (1993). *Gender and conversational interaction*. Oxford, UK: Oxford University Press.

Tannen, D. (1994). *Gender and discourse*. Oxford, UK: Oxford University Press.

Thorne, B., & Henley, N. (Eds.). (1975). *Language and sex: Difference and dominance*. Rowley, MA: Newbury House.

Tseelon, E. (1995). *The masque of femininity*. London: Sage.

Turkle, S. (1995). *Life on the screen: Identity in the age of the Internet*. New York: Simon & Schuster.

Turner, V. (1982). *From ritual to theatre*. New York: Performing Arts. Journal Publications.

Unger, R. K., & Crawford, M. (1992). *Women and gender: A feminist psychology*. Philadelphia: Temple University Press.

van Gelder, L. (1986). The strange case of the electronic lover. In G. Gumpert & S. L. Fish (Eds.), *Talking to strangers: Mediated therapeutic communication* (pp. 128–142). Norwood, NJ: Ablex.

van Lenning, A., & Maas, S. (1996, February). *Is womanliness nothing but a masquerade?* Paper presented at the Conference on Masquerade and Gendered Identity, Venice, Italy.

Werry, C. C. (1996). Linguistic and interactional features of Internet Relay Chat. In S. C. Herring (Ed.), *Computer-mediated communication: Linguistic, social, and cross-cultural perspectives* (pp. 47–64). Philadelphia: John Benjamins.

Whittle, S. (1996). Gender fucking or fucking gender: Current cultural contributions to theories of gender blending. In R. Ekin &

D. King (Eds.), *Blending genders: Social aspects of cross-dressing and sex-changing* (pp. 196–214). New York: Routledge.

Wikan, U. (1982). The Xanith: A third gender role? In U. Wikan (Ed.), *Behind the veil in Arabia: Women in Oman* (pp. 168–186). Chicago: University of Chicago Press.

Wu, G. (1993). *Cross-gender communication in cyberspace.* Unpublished manuscript, Simon Fraser University, Canada. Available: URL gopher://english.hss.cmu.edu/

5

GENDER AND RACE

THE GIRLS OF GEN X

Barbara Dafoe Whitehead

All is not well with the women of Generation X.

Consider the evidence: Close to 40 percent of college women are frequent binge drinkers, a behavior related to date rapes and venereal disease. Young women suffer higher levels of depression, suicidal thoughts and attempts than men from early adolescence on. Between 1980 and '92, the rate of completed suicides more than tripled among white girls and doubled among black girls. For white women between 15 and 24, suicide is the third leading cause of death. And there is evidence that young women are less happy today than 20 years ago. Using data from a survey of high school seniors, sociologist Norval D. Glenn has tracked the trends of reported happiness for young men and women. Since 1977, the "happiness index" has been trending downward for young women. Moreover, this decline is specific to girls. Young men's reported happiness has risen slightly over the same Time. Gen X women seem to experience the greatest discontent in two areas: Men, and their own bodies. Young women can find sex easily, but they have a hard time finding a caring and sexually faithful partner who will share their lives. Marline Pearson, who teaches at a large community college in Madison, Wisconsin, recently asked her women students to identify the greatest obstacle facing women today. The difficulty of "finding and keeping a loving partner" topped the list, outranking obstacles such as job discrimination, sexual harassment in the workplace, and domestic violence. In addition to being disappointed in their intimate relationships with men, women are discontented with their own bodies. Healthy young women of normal weight describe themselves as fat or "gross." At puberty or even earlier, girls begin restricting what they eat. Two-thirds of ninth-grade girls report attempts to lose weight in the previous month. Of course, dieting is not new, but Gen X women do more than watch calories. Some starve themselves. Others eat but are afraid to keep food in their body. Instead, they chew their food and spit it out, vomit it up, or purge it with laxatives. Even more widespread than eating disorders is disordered eating, the restrictive and obsessive monitoring of food consumption. According to some experts, most college women today suffer from disordered eating. Indeed, it is the rare college or university today that does not have at least one specialist in eating disturbances on its counseling staff. According to one survey, the number-one wish among young women, outranking the desire to end homelessness, poverty, or racism, is to get and stay thin.

These conditions afflict some of the most privileged young 3 women of the generation. This comes as a shock to older, baby-boom women. After all, college-educated Gen X women—the first full beneficiaries of the achievements of the women's movement—have grown up with more freedom, opportunity and choice than their mothers or grandmothers. More to the point, they have been the beneficiaries of what might be called the girlhood project: the systematic and self-conscious effort to change the culture and prepare girls for lives as liberated, self-determined individuals with successful careers, sexual freedoms, and nearly limitless personal choice.

As a mother raising daughters in the 1970s and '80s, I remember 4 the heady sense of possibility that accompanied the girlhood project. Sons were sons, but daughters were a social experiment. We gave them books like Marlo Thomas's *Free To Be You and Me* and read them stories in *Ms.* like "The Princess Who Could Stand on Her Own Two Feet." We dressed them in jeans and sneakers. We fought for their right to play Little League baseball. We pushed for more sex education in the schools. We urged them to please themselves rather than to please men.

Given our optimistic expectations, it is bitterly disappointing to 5 reach the '90s only to discover that young women's happiness index is falling, not rising. What is happening to our bright and talented daughters?

Several feminist writers have grappled with this question. 6 Therapist Mary Pipher was the first to describe the dark side of American girlhood in her best-selling book *Revivng Ophelia*. Pipher's case histories present a disturbing portrait of depressed and angry adolescent girls, self-mutilating, self-starving, self-loathing. Two more recent books offer a thoughtful analysis and criticism of the changing nature of American girlhood. In *Promiscuities*, her memoir of growing up fast and sexy in the '70s, Naomi Wolf describes the confused sexual awakening of privileged girls raised by self-absorbed parents too busy sampling the pleasures of the sexual revolution themselves to guide or protect their daughters. Historian Joan Jacobs Brumberg's *The Body Project: An Intimate History of Girlhood* meticulously documents the downward slide of girls' aspirations and ambitions over the past century, from improving one's character through good works to improving one's body through grueling workouts.

All three accounts point to one source of trouble: the passage 7 between girlhood and womanhood. Growing up has never been easy for girls, of course, but it is more prolonged and perilous than ever before. Puberty can begin as early as eight; first sexual intercourse commonly occurs between 15 and 17; and women remain single and sexually active into their middle or late twenties. Forty-five percent of women who came of age in the 1950s and '60s were still virgins at age 19, and for many of those 19-year-old women, their first sexual intercourse occurred on their wedding night. But only 17 percent of women who came of age in the 1970s and '80s were virgins at 19. Since many Gen X women postpone marriage until their late twenties, few are likely to be virgins on their wedding night. As a consequence, girls are exposed to the problems associated with unmarried sex at an earlier age and for a longer period of time than a generation ago.

A rough consensus exists on some key factors that make coming 8 of age more difficult for girls today: a cultural emphasis on thinness which makes the normal weight gains of puberty a source of anxiety and self-loathing; a media saturated with sexually explicit images and misogynistic messages; the sexual revolution and the availability of the Pill; which relieved men of any significant burden of responsibility for the negative consequences of unmarried sex; the high rate of family breakup and dysfunction; and the erosion of adult supervision. Puberty is now fraught with danger and anxiety.

Young girls are now at greater risk for early and traumatic sexu- 9 alization, often by adult men. According to Brumberg, there have also been dramatic shifts in the social controls governing the sexuality of adolescent girls. Professional providers of contraceptive and abortion services have replaced mothers as the main source of authority on sexual matters. This shift has contributed to the demoralization of female sexuality and the decline in chastity.

At age 15, Naomi Wolf tells us, she followed the responsible, 10 "healthy," medically approved approach to getting rid of her virginity. With her boyfriend, she went to a clinic to be fitted for a diaphragm, a business "easier than getting a learner's permit to drive a car." Yet as she prepared for the procedure, she missed a sense of occasion. "It was weird to have these adults just hand you the keys to the kingdom, ask 'Any questions?,' wave and return to their paperwork.... The end of our virginity passed unmarked," she writes, "neither mourned or celebrated."

Both Brumberg and Wolf are critical of the medicalization of 11 girls' sexuality, with its emphasis on sexual health and self-management. (In the words of one sex education book, the goal for girls is to stay "healthy, safe, and in charge.") This places an unsupportable burden on young girls to protect themselves from predatory males. It also neglects girls' emotional needs for affiliation and affection, as well as their desire to have their sexuality invested with some larger meaning.

These revisionist-feminist writers seek to remoralize girlhood, 12 but not with the morals of yesteryear. Instead, they call upon older women to take responsibility for (and pride in) younger womens' sexuality, and they look to senior women and especially mothers to instruct girls more actively. This advice overlooks at least one crucial point. Older women are already involved in shaping the passage to womanhood and have been for more than 20 years. It is feminist women who write and edit books and magazines for teen girls. It is feminist women who have fought for abortion rights and the end to parental consent laws for girls. It is feminist women who have championed the right of girls to be as sexually free as boys. In short, these older women are the authors of the girlhood project. Are they now the right parties to repair the damage done?

The girlhood project was rooted in rebellion against traditional 13 conceptions of girlhood. According to feminist critics, earlier generations of girls were raised primarily to be wives and mothers. From puberty on, parents taught daughters to be modest, nice, nurturing, accomplished in the domestic arts, and virginal. Since a young woman's virginity was a moral as well as a physical condition, family and church conspired to keep women pure.

Whether this is actually a fair summary of prevailing American 14 sex roles prior to the 1960s is dubious. Even in the 1830s, Alexis de Tocqueville commented that Americans "have calculated that there was little chance of repressing in woman the most tyrannical passions of the human heart and that it was a safer policy to teach her to control them herself. Unable to prevent her chastity from being often in danger, they want her to know how to defend herself, and they count on the strength of her free determination more than on safeguards which have been shaken or overthrown.... . Unable or unwilling to keep a girl in perpetual ignorance, they are in a hurry to give her precocious knowledge of everything."

In any case, the activists who undertook the girlhood project 15 declared war on what they viewed as Victorian double standards for boys and girls, which they blamed for unhappy marriages and unfulfilled female desires. Feminists called instead for a new single sexual standard—based on traditional boyhood. In their play and pursuits, little girls were to be made more like boys. Among liberal elites, a traditionally feminine daughter became a mild social embarrassment, while a feisty tomboy daughter was a source of pride.

In everything from sports to sex, girls gained experiences that 16 were once off-limits. Twenty-five years ago, only one in 27 high school girls participated in team sports. By 1994, one in three did. A copy-the-boys approach was also applied to sexuality. Increasingly, the timing of girls' sexual awakening resembled boys. Today, the most frequent age of first intercourse is 17 for girls, 16 for boys. In frequency of intercourse and number of sexual partners, the traditional gender gap is closing as well. Modesty has also disappeared. Girls can be as profane, sexually frank, and "horny" as the guys. "Girls talk in the casual, expletive-laced manner stereotypically attributed to men," one 18-year-old college male writes. "Sex is discussed in all its variations, and bizarre or deviant sexual practices are often explored. This sort of talk is considered 'flirting'."

Amidst its success at ending different standards for the sexes, the 17 girlhood project has created new discontents. For one thing, it contributes to girls' unhappiness with their bodies. The tomboy ideal is demanding. It favors the few girls who are naturally wiry and athletic, and leaves the majority of girls displeased with their own shapes. The rapturous acclaim for tiny Olympic gymnasts and lithe skaters gives nonathletic girls still another reason to feel disappointed in their normal forms.

The more masculine body ideal shifts the locus of body shame 18 from sexual organs to more visible body parts. Today's college women know how to find their clitoris in a mirror, but they can't bear to look at their "thunder thighs." Fashion magazines, which girls begin to read at age nine or ten and continue to consult well into their 20s, provoke body shame. Virtually all these magazines send one clear message: Your body is a mess. For example, the cover of the

December 1997 *Jump*, a magazine for young teens, features stories entitled, "Body Bummers: How to go from feeling flawed to fab" and "Sizing up boobs." Such magazines tell girls to like themselves, whatever their size or shape, but they only feature flat-chested models who are six feet tall and 105 pounds. Indeed, a recurrent rumor among teenage girls is that these models are really boys.

Girls respond to body shame with rigid technocratic monitoring [19] of their bodies. Again the strenuous pursuit of feminine virtue has not disappeared but shifted location. The virtue of staying sexually pure has been replaced by the virtue of staying physically fit. In my corner of western Massachusetts, swarms of college women descend on the local health club each fall. They work out in the weight room or on the treadmills, their pony tails bobbing, their arms pumping, their faces sweaty and serious. Some read fashion magazines as they work out.

It does not take a degree in cultural anthropology to figure out [20] that more is going on here than mere exercise. In girl culture today, "working out" is the new self-purification ritual, deeply invested with positive moral meaning. Good girls work out. Bad girls let themselves go. In the same way, eating has become a means of self-purification, and food itself has been moralized. There are good foods that one takes into the body and bad foods that one avoids or throws up. This helps explain why so many college women see "bad" foods as far more dangerous than drugs or alcohol, and why young women who drink and take recreational drugs will simultaneously refuse to eat anything but "pure" pesticide free, fat-free organic food. Food is entirely divorced from pleasure and sociability while the other ingested substances are not.

If the girlhood project leads young women on a quest for a mas- [21] culinized body, it also sets them on the path toward a more masculinized emotional life. There is now a single sex standard for men and women, but it favors Hugh Hefner, not Betty Friedan.

As much as young women's sexual lives resemble men's in the [22] timing of first sex and the number of sex partners, their reasons for having sex remain very different. The nation's most comprehensive and up-to-date sex survey reports that 48 percent of women have intercourse for the first time out of "affection for their partner," compared to only 25 percent of men. The researchers add, "Young women often go along with intercourse the first time, finding little physical pleasure in it, and a substantial number report being forced to have intercourse. These facts reflect the dramatic costs for young

women, and they seem to be increasing as young women have intercourse earlier in the life course."

Even when young women deliberately set out to lose their vir- 23
ginity, they often experience feelings of sadness, emptiness, and dis-
appointment afterward. Women may want affection, tenderness, and
commitment in their relationships, but what they actually get is
"more naked, loss-filled sex," says Warren Schumacher, who teaches
courses in marriage and the family at the University of
Massachusetts. Thus, though the girlhood project prepares girls for
sex, it says nothing to them about love.

With the decoupling of sex and love, intense passion and 24
romance are vanishing. Loveless sex has become a routine pleasure
of the single life, on a par with a good movie. Sexless love is also part
of singlehood. According to psychologist Joanna Gutmann, a coun-
selor at the University of Chicago, asexual couplings are increasingly
common. Gen X men and women may share beds without ever having sex, or they may start out in a sexual relationship and then eventually shift to a comfy, asexual living-together relationship for the
sake of companionship and convenience. Passionate, romantic love
between young men and women is increasingly rare, says Gutmann.

By the time they reach their late twenties, many educated 25
women in urban areas complain that all the good men are "taken" (or
not available because they are gay). Some single women find it easier to hook up with different people for different purposes. "It does-
n't make sense to rely on one person to meet all your needs," one
28-year-old woman told me. "Our generation diversifies. We might
have one person for sex, one to go out club-hopping, another to share
thoughts and feelings." Comradeship has replaced courtship and
marriage as the preferred path to intimacy. To use a political
metaphor, the aspiration to union has been abandoned for the more
modest goal of confederacy.

Two decades after the girlhood project began, it may be judged 26
not only by its aspirations but also by its decidedly mixed results. In
important respects, it has improved the lot of girls. Adolescent girls
now receive more serious mentoring attention from important men
in their lives, including fathers, teachers, and coaches. Their participation in sports prepares them for a work world still largely shaped
by male codes of conduct rooted in competition, combat, and con-
quest. More importantly, they are no longer bound by the marriage-
and-motherhood script. They are free to follow their own desires as
they make choices about their work and private lives.

At the same time, the girlhood project has shortchanged young 27
women. The passage from girlhood to womanhood now entails a
remarkably strenuous effort to transcend biology. Most girls are not
cut out to be tomboys forever. Too often now, normal female physical and psychological maturation is taken as a problem, a worrisome
sign that girls are "falling behind boys."

Today, all that is naturally womanly—especially anything related 28
to childbearing—is treated by elites as something to be managed,
minimized, and somehow overcome. Nearly all women still want
motherhood, but they have grown up with the idea that it is a trauma
that must be "worked into" a career. The only trouble-free times in
the female life course are now defined as the periods when women
are least connected to their womanliness: in childhood and again in
old age. A woman's life between ages 10 and 60 has been medicalized
and problematized, with a host of products and technologies like
birth control and abortion, hormone replacement therapy, and cosmetic surgery being offered to ward off or manage what is natural. Is
it any wonder that Gen X women look at adult life with a measure of
fear and trembling?

The attempt to remake American girlhood is deeply connected to 29
feminist aspirations. So how are feminists responding to signs of
trouble popping up among Generation Xers? Many are ringing alarm
bells—and blaming society or men. Others are urging their fellow
feminists to offer more personal guidance to the young. Liberal
women, say Brumberg and others, must make a new commitment to
girl advocacy.

More mentoring is a worthwhile goal, but the state of American 30
girlhood won't improve unless older feminists acknowledge their
own responsibility for creating some of the difficulties today's young
women face. To begin, women may have to confront their own anxieties about body image. Many American girls now grow up with
mothers who are dieting, working out, and always complaining
about their bodies. Indeed, it is often mothers who feel shame over
their daughters' weight gains in puberty and rush their 11-year-olds
to a fat camp or a pediatrician for a medically supervised diet.

Older feminist women, not the patriarchy, also edit the fashion 31
magazines girls so eagerly consult. Nowhere else on a newsstand
will you find as much body worship and emphasis on dress and dieting, or as many models made up like drug-addled prostitutes, or as
many articles romanticizing casual sex. The same magazines are
obsessed with money, things, and the trappings of celebrity. They
assume every girl is focused on her self and her sex life, rather than

her family and community, and they ignore any topic of civic, religious, or intellectual seriousness.

In addition, the firsthand models that today's girls grow up with are too often no more responsible or inspiring than this magazine fare. Revisionist feminists themselves acknowledge that it is the nice progressive parents of Gen Xers who turned self-actualization, divorce, live-in lovers, the drug habit (stretching from pot to Prozac), latch-key childhood, New Age therapies, and feel-good morals into mass phenomena.

Older women who aspire to be advocates to today's girls ought to consult the desires of the girls themselves. They will find that, more than sex, girls are interested in love and the business of finding a male worthy of love. Contemporary liberal institutions give these girls hundreds of books and articles devoted to the mechanics of sex, and many warnings about the dangers of penises not wearing condoms, but almost no information about how to make a life with the boys attached to them.

Older women must recognize that their feminist critique of 1950s girlhood, which inspired the effort to remake female upbringing, may not fit the realities of girls' lives now. Maybe the problem then was the tyranny of the feminine mystique. But the solution today is not a more unnatural and therefore even more tyrannical masculine mystique.

MARKED WOMEN
Deborah Tannen

Some years ago I was at a small working conference of four women and eight men. Instead of concentrating on the discussion I found myself looking at the three other women at the table, thinking how each had a different style and how each style was coherent.

One woman had dark brown hair in a classic style, a cross between Cleopatra and Plain Jane. The severity of her straight hair was softened by wavy bangs and ends that turned under. Because she was beautiful, the effect was more Cleopatra than plain.

The second woman was older, full of dignity and composure. Her hair was cut in a fashionable style that left her with only one eye, thanks to a side part that let a curtain of hair fall across half her face. As she looked down to read her prepared paper, the hair robbed her of bifocal vision and created a barrier between her and the listeners.

The third woman's hair was wild, a frosted blond avalanche falling over and beyond her shoulders. When she spoke she frequently tossed her head, calling attention to her hair and away from her lecture.

Then there was makeup. The first woman wore facial cover that made her skin smooth and pale, a black line under each eye and mascara that darkened already dark lashes. The second wore only a light gloss on her lips and a hint of shadow on her eyes. The third had blue bands under her eyes, dark blue shadow, mascara, bright red lipstick and rouge; her fingernails flashed red.

I considered the clothes each woman had worn during the three days of the conference: In the first case, man-tailored suits in primary colors with solid-color blouses. In the second, casual but stylish black T-shirts, a floppy collarless jacket and baggy slacks or a skirt in neutral colors. The third wore a sexy jump suit; tight sleeveless jersey and tight yellow slacks; a dress with gaping armholes and an indulged tendency to fall off one shoulder.

Shoes? No. 1 wore string sandals with medium heels; No. 2, sensible, comfortable walking shoes; No. 3, pumps with spike heels. You can fill in the jewelry, scarves, shawls, sweaters—or lack of them.

As I amused myself finding coherence in these styles, I suddenly wondered why I was scrutinizing only the women. I scanned the eight men at the table. And then I knew why I wasn't studying them. The men's styles were unmarked.

The term "marked" is a staple of linguistic theory. It refers to the 9 way language alters the base meaning of a word by adding a linguistic particle that has no meaning on its own. The unmarked form of a word carries the meaning that goes without saying—what you think of when you're not thinking anything special.

The unmarked tense of verbs in English is the present—for 10 example, *visit*. To indicate past, you mark the verb by adding ed to yield *visited*. For future, you add a word: *will visit*. Nouns are presumed to be singular until marked for plural, typically by adding *s* or *es*, so *visit* becomes *visits* and *dish* becomes *dishes*.

The unmarked forms of most English words also convey "male." 11 Being male is the unmarked case. Endings like *ess* and *ette* mark words as "female." Unfortunately, they also tend to mark them for frivolousness. Would you feel safe entrusting your life to a doctorette? Alfre Woodard, who was an Oscar nominee for best supporting actress, says she identifies herself as an actor because "actresses worry about eyelashes and cellulite, and women who are actors worry about the characters we are playing." Gender markers pick up extra meanings that reflect common associations with the female gender: not quite serious, often sexual.

Each of the women at the conference had to make decisions 12 about hair, clothing, makeup and accessories, and each decision carried meaning. Every style available to us was marked. The men in our group had made decisions, too, but the range from which they chose was incomparably narrower. Men can choose styles that are marked, but they don't have to, and in this group none did. Unlike the women, they had the option of being unmarked.

Take the men's hair styles. There was no marine crew cut or oily 13 longish hair falling into eyes, no asymmetrical, two-tiered construction to swirl over a bald top. One man was unabashedly bald; the others had hair of standard length, parted on one side, in natural shades of brown or gray or graying. Their hair obstructed no views, left little to toss or push back or run fingers through and, consequently, needed and attracted no attention. A few men had beards. In a business setting, beards might be marked. In this academic gathering, they weren't.

There could have been a cowboy shirt with string tie or a three- 14 piece suit or a necklaced hippie in jeans. But there wasn't. All eight men wore brown or blue slacks and nondescript shirts of light colors.

No man wore sandals or boots; their shoes were dark, closed, comfortable and flat. In short, unmarked.

Although no man wore makeup, you couldn't say the men 15 didn't wear makeup in the sense that you could say a woman didn't wear makeup. For men, no makeup is unmarked.

I asked myself what style we women could have adopted that 16 would have been unmarked, like the men's. The answer was none. There is no unmarked woman.

There is no woman's hair style that can be called standard, that 17 says nothing about her. The range of women's hair styles is staggering, but a woman whose hair has no particular style is perceived as not caring about how she looks, which can disqualify her for many positions, and will subtly diminish her as a person in the eyes of some.

Women must choose between attractive shoes and comfortable 18 shoes. When our group made an unexpected trek, the woman who wore flat, laced shoes arrived first. Last to arrive was the woman in spike heels, shoes in hand and a handful of men around her.

If a woman's clothing is tight or revealing (in other words, sexy), 19 it sends a message—an intended one of wanting to be attractive, but also a possibly unintended one of availability. If her clothes are not sexy, that too sends a message, lent meaning by the knowledge that they could have been. There are thousands of cosmetic products from which women can choose and myriad ways of applying them. Yet no makeup at all is anything but unmarked. Some men see it as a hostile refusal to please them.

Women can't even fill out a form without telling stories about 20 themselves. Most forms give four titles to choose from. "Mr." carries no meaning other than that the respondent is male. But a woman who checks "Mrs." or "Miss" communicates not only whether she has been married but also whether she has conservative tastes in forms of address—and probably other conservative values as well. Checking "Ms." declines to let on about marriage (checking "Mr." declines nothing since nothing was asked), but it also marks her as either liberated or rebellious, depending on the observer's attitudes and assumptions.

I sometimes try to duck these variously marked choices by giving 21 my title as "Dr."—and in so doing risk marking myself as either uppity (hence sarcastic responses like "Excuse me!") or an overachiever (hence reactions of congratulatory surprise like "Good for you!").

All married women's surnames are marked. If a woman takes 22 her husband's name, she announces to the world that she is married and has traditional values. To some it will indicate that she is less herself, more identified by her husband's identity. If she does not take her husband's name, this too is marked, seen as worthy of comment: she has done something; she has "kept her own name." A man is never said to have "kept his own name" because it never occurs to anyone that he might have given it up. For him using his own name is unmarked.

A married woman who wants to have her cake and eat it too may   23 use her surname plus his, with or without a hyphen. But this too announces her marital status and often results in a tongue-tying string. In a list (Harvey O'Donovan, Jonathan Feldman, Stephanie Woodbury McGillicutty), the woman's multiple name stands out. It is marked.

I have never been inclined toward biological explanations of gen-   24 der differences in language, but I was intrigued to see Ralph Fasold bring biological phenomena to bear on the question of linguistic marking in his book *The Sociolinguistics of Language*. Fasold stresses that language and culture are particularly unfair in treating women as the marked case because biologically it is the male that is marked. While two X chromosomes make a female, two Y chromosomes make nothing. Like the linguistic markers *s*, *es* or *ess*, the Y chromosome doesn't "mean" anything unless it is attached to a root form—an X chromosome.

Developing this idea elsewhere, Fasold points out that girls are   25 born with fully female bodies, while boys are born with modified female bodies. He invites men who doubt this to lift up their shirts and contemplate why they have nipples.

In his book, Fasold notes "a wide range of facts which demon-   26 strates that female is the unmarked sex." For example, he observes that there are a few species that produce only females, like the whip-tail lizard. Thanks to parthenogenesis, they have no trouble having as many daughters as they like. There are no species, however, that produce only males. This is no surprise, since any such species would become extinct in its first generation.

Fasold is also intrigued by species that produce individuals not   27 involved in reproduction, like honeybees and leaf-cutter ants. Reproduction is handled by the queen and a relatively few males; the workers are sterile females. "Since they do not reproduce," Fasold says, "there is no reason for them to be one sex or the other, so they default, so to speak, to female."

Fasold ends his discussion of these matters by pointing out that   28 if language reflected biology, grammar books would direct us to use "she" to include males and females and "he" only for specifically male referents. But they don't. They tell us that "he" means "he or she," and that "she" is used only if the referent is specifically female.

This use of "he" as the sex-indefinite pronoun is an innovation introduced into English by grammarians in the 18th and 19th centuries,
according to Peter Muhlhausler and Rom Harre in "Pronouns and
People." From at least about 1500, the correct sex-indefinite pronoun
was "they," as it still is in casual spoken English. In other words, the
female was declared by grammarians to be the marked case.

Writing this article may mark me not as a writer, not as a linguist, 29
not as an analyst of human behavior, but as a feminist—which will
have positive or negative, but in any case powerful, connotations for
readers. Yet I doubt that anyone reading Ralph Fasold's book would
put that label on him.

I discovered the markedness inherent in the very topic of gender 30
after writing a book on differences in conversational style based on
geographical region, ethnicity, class, age and gender. When I was
interviewed, the vast majority of journalists wanted to talk about the
differences between women and men. While I thought I was simply
describing what I observed—something I had learned to do as a
researcher—merely mentioning women and men marked me as a
feminist for some.

When I wrote a book devoted to gender differences in ways of 31
speaking, I sent the manuscript to five male colleagues, asking them
to alert me to any interpretation, phrasing or wording that might
seem unfairly negative toward men. Even so, when the book came
out, I encountered responses like that of the television talk show host
who, after interviewing me, turned to the audience and asked if they
thought I was male-bashing.

Leaping upon a poor fellow who affably nodded in agreement, 32
she made him stand and asked, "Did what she said accurately
describe you?" "Oh, yes," he answered. "That's me exactly." "And
what she said about women—does that sound like your wife?" "Oh
yes," he responded. "That's her exactly." "Then why do you think
she's male-bashing?" He answered, with disarming honesty,
"Because she's a woman and she's saying things about men."

To say anything about women and men without marking oneself 33
as either feminist or anti-feminist, male-basher or apologist for men
seems as impossible for a woman as trying to get dressed in the
morning without inviting interpretations of her character.

Sitting at the conference table musing on these matters, I felt sad 34
to think that we women didn't have the freedom to be unmarked that
the men sitting next to us had. Some days you just want to get
dressed and go about your business. But if you're a woman, you
can't, because there is no unmarked woman.

JUST WALK ON BY

Brent Staples

My first victim was a woman—white, well dressed, probably in 1
her early twenties. I came upon her late one evening on a deserted
street in Hyde Park, a relatively affluent neighborhood in an otherwise mean, impoverished section of Chicago. As I swung onto the
avenue behind her, there seemed to be a discreet, uninflammatory
distance between us. Not so. She cast back a worried glance. To her,
the youngish black man—a broad six feet two inches with a beard
and billowing hair, both hands shoved into the pockets of a bulky
military jacket—seemed menacingly close. After a few more quick
glimpses, she picked up her pace and was soon running in earnest.
Within seconds she disappeared into a cross street.

That was more than a decade ago. I was 22 years old, a graduate 2
student newly arrived at the University of Chicago. It was in the echo
of that terrified woman's footfalls that I first began to know the
unwieldy inheritance I'd come into—the ability to alter public space
in ugly ways. It was clear that she thought herself the quarry of a
mugger, a rapist, or worse. Suffering a bout of insomnia, however, I
was stalking sleep, not defenseless wayfarers. As a softy who is
scarcely able to take a knife to a raw chicken—let alone hold it to a
person's throat—I was surprised, embarrassed, and dismayed all at
once. Her flight made me feel like an accomplice in tyranny. It also
made it clear that I was indistinguishable from the muggers who
occasionally seeped into the area from the surrounding ghetto. That
first encounter, and those that followed, signified that a vast, unnerv-
ing gulf lay between nighttime pedestrians—particularly women—
and me. And I soon gathered that being perceived as dangerous is a
hazard in itself. I only needed to turn a corner into a dicey situation,
or crowd some frightened, armed person in a foyer somewhere, or
make an errant move after being pulled over by a policeman. Where
fear and weapons meet—and they often do in urban America—there
is always the possibility of death.

In that first year, my first away from my hometown, I was to 3
become thoroughly familiar with the language of fear. At dark, shadowy intersections in Chicago, I could cross in front of a car stopped
at a traffic light and elicit the *thunk, thunk, thunk, thunk* of the driver—
black, white, male, or female—hammering down the door locks. On
less traveled streets after dark, I grew accustomed to but never com-

fortable with people who crossed to the other side of the street rather than pass me. Then there were the standard unpleasantries with police, doormen, bouncers, cab drivers, and others whose business it is to screen out troublesome individuals *before* there is any nastiness.

I moved to New York nearly two years ago and I have remained an avid night walker. In central Manhattan, the near-constant crowd cover minimizes tense one-on-one street encounters. Elsewhere—visiting friends in SoHo, where sidewalks are narrow and tightly spaced buildings shut out the sky—things can get very taut indeed.

Black men have a firm place in New York mugging literature. Norman Podhoretz in his famed (or infamous) 1963 essay, "My Negro Problem—And Ours," recalls growing up in terror of black males; they "were tougher than we were, more ruthless," he writes— and as an adult on the Upper West Side of Manhattan, he continues, he cannot constrain his nervousness when he meets black men on certain streets. Similarly, a decade later, the essayist and novelist Edward Hoagland extols a New York where once "Negro bitterness bore down mainly on other Negroes." Where some see mere panhandlers, Hoagland sees "a mugger who is clearly screwing up his nerve to do more than just *ask* for money." But Hoagland has "the New Yorker's quickhunch posture for broken-field maneuvering," and the bad guy swerves away.

I often witness that "hunch posture," from women after dark on the warrenlike streets of Brooklyn where I live. They seem to set their faces on neutral and, with their purse straps strung across their chests bandolier style, they forge ahead as though bracing themselves against being tackled. I understand, of course, that the danger they perceive is not a hallucination. Women are particularly vulnerable to street violence, and young black males are drastically overrepresented among the perpetrators of that violence. Yet these truths are no solace against the kind of alienation that comes of being ever the suspect, against being set apart, a fearsome entity with whom pedestrians avoid making eye contact.

It is not altogether clear to me how I reached the ripe old age of 22 without being conscious of the lethality nighttime pedestrians attributed to me. Perhaps it was because in Chester, Pennsylvania, the small, angry industrial town where I came of age in the 1960s, I was scarcely noticeable against a backdrop of gang warfare, street knifings, and murders. I grew up one of the good boys, had perhaps a half-dozen fist fights. In retrospect, my shyness of combat has clear sources.

Many things go into the making of a young thug. One of those 8
things is the consummation of the male romance with the power to
intimidate. An infant discovers that random flailings send the baby
bottle flying out of the crib and crashing to the floor. Delighted, the
joyful babe repeats those motions again and again, seeking to dupli-
cate the feat. Just so, I recall the points at which some of my boyhood
friends were finally seduced by the perception of themselves as
tough guys. When a mark cowered and surrendered his money without resistance, myth and reality merged—and paid off. It is, after all,
only manly to embrace the power to frighten and intimidate. We, as
men, are not supposed to give an inch of our lane on the highway; we
are to seize the fighter's edge in work and in play and even in love;
we are to be valiant in the face of hostile forces.

Unfortunately, poor and powerless young men seem to take all 9
this nonsense literally. As a boy, I saw countless tough guys locked
away; I have since buried several, too. They were babies, really—a
teenage cousin, a brother of 22, a childhood friend in his mid-
twenties—all gone down in episodes of bravado played out in the
streets. I came to doubt the virtues of intimidation early on. I chose,
perhaps even unconsciously, to remain a shadow—timid, but a
survivor.

The fearsomeness mistakenly attributed to me in public places 10
often has a perilous flavor. The most frightening of these confusions
occurred in the late 1970s and early 1980s when I worked as a journalist in Chicago. One day, rushing into the office of a magazine I was
writing for with a deadline story in hand, I was mistaken for a bur-
glar. The office manager called security and, with an ad hoc posse,
pursued me through the labyrinthine halls, nearly to my editor's
door. I had no way of proving who I was. I could only move briskly
toward the company of someone who knew me.

Another time I was on assignment for a local paper and killing 11
time before an interview. I entered a jewelry store on the city's affluent Near North Side. The proprietor excused herself and returned
with an enormous red Doberman pinscher straining at the end of a
leash. She stood, the dog extended toward me, silent to my questions,
her eyes bulging nearly out of her head. I took a cursory look around,
nodded, and bade her good night. Relatively speaking, however, I
never fared as badly as another black male journalist. He went to
nearby Waukegan, Illinois, a couple of summers ago to work on a
story about a murderer who was born there. Mistaking the reporter
for the killer, police hauled him from his car at gunpoint and but for

his press credentials would probably have tried to book him. Such episodes are not uncommon. Black men trade tales like this all the time.

In "My Negro Problem—And Ours," Podhoretz writes that the 12 hatred he feels for blacks makes itself known to him through a variety of avenues—one being his discomfort with that "special brand of paranoid touchiness" to which he says blacks are prone. No doubt he is speaking here of black men. In time, I learned to smother the rage I felt at so often being taken for a criminal. Not to do so would surely have led to madness—via that special "paranoid touchiness" that so annoyed Podhoretz at the time he wrote the essay.

I began to take precautions to make myself less threatening. I 13 move about with care, particularly late in the evening. I give a wide berth to nervous people on subway platforms during the wee hours, particularly when I have exchanged business clothes for jeans. If I happen to be entering a building behind some people who appear skittish, I may walk by, letting them clear the lobby before I return, so as not to seem to be following them. I have been calm and extremely congenial on those rare occasions when I've been pulled over by the police.

And on late-evening constitutionals along streets less traveled 14 by, I employ what has proved to be an excellent tension-reducing measure: I whistle melodies from Beethoven and Vivaldi and the more popular classical composers. Even steely New Yorkers hunching toward nighttime destinations seem to relax, and occasionally they even join in the tune. Virtually everybody seems to sense that a mugger wouldn't be warbling bright, sunny selections from Vivaldi's *Four Seasons*. It is my equivalent of the cowbell that hikers wear when they know they are in bear country.

6

LITERATURE AND LANGUAGE

MOTHER TONGUE

Amy Tan

I am not a scholar of English or literature. I cannot give you much 1
more than personal opinions on the English language and its variations in this country or others.

I am a writer. And by that definition, I am someone who has 2
always loved language. I am fascinated by language in daily life. I
spend a great deal of my time thinking about the power of language—the way it can evoke an emotion, a visual image, a complex
idea, or a simple truth. Language is the tool of my trade. And I use
them all—all the Englishes I grew up with.

Recently, I was made keenly aware of the different Englishes I 3
do use. I was giving a talk to a large group of people, the same talk I
had already given to half a dozen other groups. The nature of the talk
was about my writing, my life, and my book, *The Joy Luck Club*. The
talk was going along well enough, until I remembered one major difference that made the whole talk sound wrong. My mother was in
the room. And it was perhaps the first time she had heard me give a
lengthy speech, using the kind of English I have never used with her.
I was saying things like, "The intersection of memory upon imagination" and "There is an aspect of my fiction that relates to
thus-and-thus"—a speech filled with carefully wrought grammatical
phrases, burdened, it suddenly seemed to me, with nominalized
forms, past perfect tenses, conditional phrases, all the forms of standard English that I had learned in school and through books, the
forms of English I did not use at home with my mother.

Just last week, I was walking down the street with my mother, 4
and I again found myself conscious of the English I was using, and

the English I do use with her. We were talking about the price of new and used furniture and I heard myself saying this: "Not waste money that way." My husband was with us as well, and he didn't notice any switch in my English. And then I realized why. It's because over the twenty years we've been together I've often used that same kind of English with him, and sometimes he even uses it with me. It has become our language of intimacy, a different sort of English that relates to family talk, the language I grew up with.

So you'll have some idea of what this family talk I heard sounds 5 like, I'll quote what my mother said during a recent conversation which I videotaped and then transcribed. During this conversation, my mother was talking about a political gangster in Shanghai who had the same last name as her family's, Du, and how the gangster in his early years wanted to be adopted by her family, which was rich by comparison. Later, the gangster became more powerful, far richer than my mother's family, and one day showed up at my mother's wedding to pay his respects. Here's what she said in part: "Du Yusong having business like fruit stand. Like off the street kind. He is Du like Du Zong—but not Tsung-ming Island people. The local people call putong, the river east side, he belong to that side local people. The man want to ask Du Zong father take him in like become own family. Du Zong father wasn't look down on him, but didn't take seriously, until that man big like become a mafia. Now important person, very hard to inviting him. Chinese way, came only to show respect, don't stay for dinner. Respect for making big celebration, he shows up. Mean gives lots of respect. Chinese custom. Chinese social life that way. If too important won't have to stay too long. He come to my wedding. I didn't see, I heard it. I gone to boy's side, they have YMCA dinner. Chinese age I was nineteen."

You should know that my mother's expressive command of 6 English belies how much she actually understands. She reads the Forbes report, listens to *Wall Street Week*, converses daily with her stockbroker, reads all of Shirley MacLaine's[1] books with ease—all kinds of things I can't begin to understand. Yet some of my friends tell me they understand 50 percent of what my mother says. Some say they understand 80 to 90 percent. Some say they understand none of it, as if she were speaking pure Chinese. But to me, my mother's English is perfectly clear, perfectly natural. It's my mother tongue. Her language, as I hear it, is vivid, direct, full of observation and

---

[1] Actress known for her autobiographical books, in which she traces her many past lives.

imagery. That was the language that helped shape the way I saw things, expressed things, made sense of the world.

Lately, I've been giving more thought to the kind of English my mother speaks. Like others, I have described it to people as "broken" or "fractured" English. But I wince when I say that. It has always bothered me that I can think of no way to describe it other than "broken," as if it were damaged and needed to be fixed, as if it lacked a certain wholeness and soundness. I've heard other terms used, "limited English," for example. But they seem just as bad, as if everything is limited, including people's perceptions of the limited English speaker.

I know this for a fact, because when I was growing up, my mother's "limited" English limited *my* perception of her. I was ashamed of her English. I believed that her English reflected the quality of what she had to say. That is, because she expressed them imperfectly her thoughts were imperfect. And I had plenty of empirical evidence to support me: the fact that people in department stores, at banks, and at restaurants did not take her seriously, did not give her good service, pretended not to understand her, or even acted as if they did not hear her.

My mother has long realized the limitations of her English as well. When I was fifteen, she used to have me call people on the phone to pretend I was she. In this guise, I was forced to ask for information or even to complain and yell at people who had been rude to her. One time it was a call to her stockbroker in New York. She had cashed out her small portfolio and it just so happened we were going to go to New York the next week, our very first trip outside California. I had to get on the phone and say in an adolescent voice that was not very convincing, "This is Mrs. Tan."

And my mother was standing in the back whispering loudly, "Why he don't send me check, already two weeks late. So mad he lie to me, losing me money."

And then I said in perfect English, "Yes, I'm getting rather concerned. You had agreed to send the check two weeks ago, but it hasn't arrived."

Then she began to talk more loudly. "What he want, I come to New York tell him front of his boss, you cheating me?" And I was trying to calm her down, make her be quiet, while telling the stockbroker, "I can't tolerate any more excuses. If I don't receive the check immediately, I am going to have to speak to your manager when I'm in New York next week." And sure enough, the following week there we were in front of this astonished stockbroker, and I was sitting there red-faced and quiet, and my mother, the real Mrs. Tan, was shouting at his boss in her impeccable broken English.

We used a similar routine just five days ago, for a situation that was far less humorous. My mother had gone to the hospital for an appointment, to find out about a benign brain tumor a CAT scan had revealed a month ago. She said she had spoken very good English, her best English, no mistakes. Still, she said, the hospital did not apologize when they said they had lost the CAT scan and she had come for nothing. She said they did not seem to have any sympathy when she told them she was anxious to know the exact diagnosis, since her husband and son had both died of brain tumors. She said they would not give her any more information until the next time and she would have to make another appointment for that. So she said she would not leave until the doctor called her daughter. She wouldn't budge. And when the doctor finally called her daughter, me, who spoke in perfect English—lo and behold—we had assurances the CAT scan would be found, promises that a conference call on Monday would be held, and apologies for any suffering my mother had gone through for a most regrettable mistake. 13

I think my mother's English almost had an effect on limiting my possibilities in life as well. Sociologists and linguists probably will tell you that a person's developing language skills are more influenced by peers. But I do think that the language spoken in the family, especially in immigrant families which are more insular, plays a large role in shaping the language of the child. And I believe that it affected my results on achievement tests, IQ tests, and the SAT. While my English skills were never judged as poor, compared to math, English could not be considered my strong suit. In grade school I did moderately well, getting perhaps B's, sometimes B-pluses, in English and scoring perhaps in the sixtieth or seventieth percentile on achievement tests. But those scores were not good enough to override the opinion that my true abilities lay in math and science, because in those areas I achieved A's and scored in the ninetieth percentile or higher. 14

This was understandable. Math is precise; there is only one correct answer. Whereas, for me at least, the answers on English tests were always a judgment call, a matter of opinion and personal experience. Those tests were constructed around items like fill-in-the-blank sentence completion, such as, "Even though Tom was _____, Mary thought he was _____." And the correct answer always seemed to be the most bland combinations of thoughts, for example, "Even though Tom was shy, Mary thought he was charming," with the grammatical structure "even though" limiting the correct answer to some sort of 15 semantic opposites, so you wouldn't get answers like, "Even though Tom was foolish, Mary thought he was ridiculous." Well, according to my mother, there were very few limitations as to what Tom could have been and what Mary might have thought of him. So I never did well on tests like that.

The same was true with word analogies, pairs of words in which 16 you were supposed to find some sort of logical, semantic relationship—for example, "*Sunset* is to *nightfall* as _____ is to _____." And here you would be presented with a list of four possible pairs, one of which showed the same kind of relationship: *red* is to *stoplight, bus* is to *arrival, chills* is to *fever, yawn* is to *boring*. Well, I could never think that way. I knew what the tests were asking, but I could not block out of my mind the images already created by the first pair, "*sunset* is to *nightfall*"—and I would see a burst of colors against a darkening sky, the moon rising, the lowering of a curtain of stars. And all the other pairs of words—red, bus, stoplight, boring—just threw up a mass of confusing images, making it impossible for me to sort out something as logical as saying: "A sunset precedes nightfall" is the same as "a chill precedes a fever." The only way I would have gotten that answer right would have been to imagine an associative situation, for example, my being disobedient and staying out past sunset, catching a chill at night, which turns into feverish pneumonia as punishment, which indeed did happen to me.

I have been thinking about all this lately, about my mother's 17 English, about achievement tests. Because lately I've been asked, as a writer, why there are not more Asian Americans represented in American literature. Why are there few Asian Americans enrolled in creative writing programs? Why do so many Chinese students go into engineering? Well, these are broad sociological questions I can't begin to answer. But I have noticed in surveys—in fact, just last week—that Asian students, as a whole, always do significantly better on math achievement tests than in English. And this makes me think that there are other Asian-American students whose English spoken in the home might also be described as "broken" or "limited." And perhaps they also have teachers who are steering them away from writing and into math and science, which is what happened to me.

Fortunately, I happen to be rebellious in nature and enjoy the chal- 18 lenge of disproving assumptions made about me. I became an English major my first year in college, after being enrolled as pre-med. I started writing nonfiction as a freelancer the week after I was told by my former boss that writing was my worst skill and I should hone my talents toward account management.

But it wasn't until 1985 that I finally began to write fiction. And 19 at first I wrote using what I thought to be wittily crafted sentences, sentences that would finally prove I had mastery over the English language. Here's an example from the first draft of a story that later made its way into *The Joy Luck Club,* but without this line: "That was my mental quandary in its nascent state." A terrible line, which I can barely pronounce.

Fortunately, for reasons I won't get into today, I later decided 20 I should envision a reader for the stories I would write. And the reader I decided upon was my mother, because these were stories about mothers. So with this reader in mind—and in fact she did read my early drafts—I began to write stories using all the Englishes I grew up with: the English I spoke to my mother, which for lack of a better term might be described as "simple"; the English she used with me, which for lack of a better term might be described as "broken"; my translation of her Chinese, which could certainly be described as "watered down"; and what I imagined to be her translation of her Chinese if she could speak in perfect English, her internal language, and for that I sought to preserve the essence, but neither an English nor a Chinese structure. I wanted to capture what language ability tests can never reveal: her intent, her passion, her imagery, the rhythms of her speech and the nature of her thoughts.

Apart from what any critic had to say about my writing, I knew 21 I had succeeded where it counted when my mother finished reading my book and gave me her verdict: "So easy to read."

WHAT WE TALK ABOUT WHEN WE TALK ABOUT LOVE

Raymond Carver

My friend Mel McGinnis was talking. Mel McGinnis is a cardiol- 1
ogist, and sometimes that gives him the right.

The four of us were sitting around his kitchen table drinking gin. 2
Sunlight filled the kitchen from the big window behind the sink.
There were Mel and me and his second wife, Teresa—Terri, we called
her—and my wife, Laura. We lived in Albuquerque then. But we
were all from somewhere else.

There was an ice bucket on the table. The gin and the tonic water 3
kept going around, and we somehow got on the subject of love. Mel
thought real love was nothing less than spiritual love. He said he'd
spent five years in a seminary before quitting to go to medical school.
He said he still looked back on those years in the seminary as the
most important years in his life.

Terri said the man she lived with before she lived with Mel loved 4
her so much he tried to kill her. Then Terri said, "He beat me up one
night. He dragged me around the living room by my ankles. He kept
saying, 'I love you, I love you, you bitch.' He went on dragging me
around the living room. My head kept knocking on things." Terri
looked around the table. "What do you do with love like that?"

She was a bone-thin woman with a pretty face, dark eyes, and 5
brown hair that hung down her back. She liked necklaces made of
turquoise, and long pendant earrings.

"My God, don't be silly. That's not love, and you know it," Mel 6
said. "I don't know what you'd call it, but I sure know you wouldn't
call it love."

"Say what you want to, but I know it was," Terri said. "It may 7
sound crazy to you, but it's true just the same. People are different,
Mel. Sure, sometimes he may have acted crazy. Okay. But he loved
me. In his own way maybe, but he loved me. There was love there,
Mel. Don't say there wasn't."

Mel let out his breath. He held his glass and turned to Laura and 8
me. "The man threatened to kill me," Mel said. He finished his drink
and reached for the gin bottle. "Terri's a romantic. Terri's of the kick-
me-so-I'll-know-you-love-me school. Terri, hon, don't look that
way." Mel reached across the table and touched Terri's cheek with his
fingers. He grinned at her.

"Now he wants to make up," Terri said.   9

"Make up what?" Mel said. "What is there to make up? I know 10
what I know. That's all."

"How'd we get started on this subject, anyway?" Terri said. She 11
raised her glass and drank from it. "Mel always has love on his
mind," she said. "Don't you, honey?" She smiled, and I thought that
was the last of it.

"I just wouldn't call Ed's behavior love. That's all I'm saying, 12
honey," Mel said. "What about you guys?" Mel said to Laura and me.
"Does that sound like love to you?"

"I'm the wrong person to ask," I said. "I didn't even know the 13
man. I've only heard his name mentioned in passing. I wouldn't
know. You'd have to know the particulars. But I think what you're
saying is that love is an absolute."

Mel said, "The kind of love I'm talking about is. The kind of love 14
I'm talking about, you don't try to kill people."

Laura said, "I don't know anything about Ed, or anything about 15
the situation. But who can judge anyone else's situation?"

I touched the back of Laura's hand. She gave me a quick smile. I 16
picked up Laura's hand. It was warm, the nails polished, perfectly
manicured. I encircled the broad wrist with my fingers, and I held
her.

"When I left, he drank rat poison," Terri said. She clasped her 17
arms with her hands. "They took him to the hospital in Santa Fe.
That's where we lived then, about ten miles out. They saved his life.
But his gums went crazy from it. I mean they pulled away from his
teeth. After that, his teeth stood out like fangs. My God," Terri said.
She waited a minute, then let go of her arms and picked up her glass.

"What people won't do!" Laura said.   18

"He's out of the action now," Mel said. "He's dead."   19

Mel handed me the saucer of limes. I took a section, squeezed it 20
over my drink, and stirred the ice cubes with my finger.

"It gets worse," Terri said. "He shot himself in the mouth. But he 21
bungled that too. Poor Ed," she said. Terri shook her head.

"Poor Ed nothing," Mel said. "He was dangerous."   22

Mel was forty-five years old. He was tall and rangy with curly 23
soft hair. His face and arms were brown from the tennis he played.
When he was sober, his gestures, all his movements, were precise,
very careful.

"He did love me though, Mel. Grant me that," Terri said. "That's 24
all I'm asking. He didn't love me the way you love me. I'm not saying that. But he loved me. You can grant me that, can't you?"

"What do you mean, he bungled it?" I said.   25

Laura leaned forward with her glass. She put her elbows on the 26
table and held her glass in both hands. She glanced from Mel to Terri
and waited with a look of bewilderment on her open face, as if
amazed that such things happened to people you were friendly with.

"How'd he bungle it when he killed himself?" I said.   27

"I'll tell you what happened," Mel said. "He took this twenty- 28
two pistol he'd bought to threaten Terri and me with. Oh, I'm serious,
the man was always threatening. You should have seen the way we
lived in those days. Like fugitives. I even bought a gun myself. Can
you believe it? A guy like me? But I did. I bought one for self-defense
and carried it in the glove compartment. Sometimes I'd have to leave
the apartment in the middle of the night. To go to the hospital, you
know? Terri and I weren't married then, and my first wife had the
house and kids, the dog, everything, and Terri and I were living in
this apartment here. Sometimes, as I say, I'd get a call in the middle
of the night and have to go in to the hospital at two or three in the
morning. It'd be dark out there in the parking lot, and I'd break into
a sweat before I could even get to my car. I never knew if he was
going to come up out of the shrubbery or from behind a car and start
shooting. I mean, the man was crazy. He was capable of wiring a
bomb, anything. He used to call my service at all hours and say he
needed to talk to the doctor, and when I'd return the call, he'd say,
'Son of a bitch, your days are numbered.' Little things like that. It was
scary, I'm telling you."

"I still feel sorry for him," Terri said.   29

"It sounds like a nightmare," Laura said. "But what exactly hap- 30
pened after he shot himself?"

Laura is a legal secretary. We'd met in a professional capacity. 31
Before we knew it, it was a courtship. She's thirty-five, three years
younger than I am. In addition to being in love, we like each other
and enjoy one another's company. She's easy to be with.

"What happened?" Laura said.   32

Mel said, "He shot himself in the mouth in his room. Someone 33
heard the shot and told the manager. They came in with a passkey,
saw what had happened, and called an ambulance. I happened to be
there when they brought him in, alive but past recall. The man lived

for three days. His head swelled up to twice the size of a normal head. I'd never seen anything like it, and I hope I never do again. Terri wanted to go in and sit with him when she found out about it. We had a fight over it. I didn't think she should see him like that. I didn't think she should see him, and I still don't."

"Who won the fight?" Laura said.   34

"I was in the room with him when he died," Terri said. "He never 35 came up out of it. But I sat with him. He didn't have anyone else."

"He was dangerous," Mel said. "If you call that love, you can 36 have it."

"It was love," Terri said. "Sure, it's abnormal in most people's 37 eyes. But he was willing to die for it. He did die for it."

"I sure as hell wouldn't call it love," Mel said. "I mean, no one 38 knows what he did it for. I've seen a lot of suicides, and I couldn't say anyone ever knew what they did it for."

Mel put his hands behind his neck and tilted his chair back. "I'm 39 not interested in that kind of love," he said. "If that's love, you can have it."

Terri said, "We were afraid. Mel even made a will out and wrote 40 to his brother in California who used to be a Green Beret. Mel told him who to look for if something happened to him."

Terri drank from her glass. She said, "But Mel's right—we lived 41 like fugitives. We were afraid. Mel was, weren't you, honey? I even called the police at one point, but they were no help. They said they couldn't do anything until Ed actually did something. Isn't that a laugh?" Terri said.

She poured the last of the gin into her glass and waggled the bot- 42 tle. Mel got up from the table and went to the cupboard. He took down another bottle.

"Well, Nick and I know what love is," Laura said. "For us, I 43 mean," Laura said. She bumped my knee with her knee. "You're supposed to say something now," Laura said, and turned her smile on me.

For an answer, I took Laura's hand and raised it to my lips. I 44 made a big production out of kissing her hand. Everyone was amused.

"We're lucky," I said.   45

"You guys," Terri said. "Stop that now. You're making me sick. 46 You're still on the honeymoon, for God's sake. You're still gaga, for crying out loud. Just wait. How long have you been together now? How long has it been? A year? Longer than a year?"

"Going on a year and a half," Laura said, flushed and smiling.   47

"Oh, now," Terri said. "Wait awhile."   48

She held her drink and gazed at Laura.   49

"I'm only kidding," Terri said.   50

Mel opened the gin and went around the table with the bottle.   51

"Here, you guys," he said. "Let's have a toast. I want to propose   52
a toast. A toast to love. To true love," Mel said.

We touched glasses.   53

"To love," we said.   54

Outside in the backyard, one of the dogs began to bark. The   55
leaves of the aspen that leaned past the window ticked against the
glass. The afternoon sun was like a presence in this room, the spa-
cious light of ease and generosity. We could have been anywhere,
somewhere enchanted. We raised our glasses again and grinned at
each other like children who had agreed on something forbidden.

"I'll tell you what real love is," Mel said. "I mean, I'll give you a   56
good example. And then you can draw your own conclusions." He
poured more gin into his glass. He added an ice cube and a sliver of
lime. We waited and sipped our drinks. Laura and I touched knees
again. I put a hand on her warm thigh and left it there.

"What do any of us really know about love?" Mel said. "It seems   57
to me we're just beginners at love. We say we love each other and we
do, I don't doubt it. I love Terri and Terri loves me, and you guys love
each other too. You know the kind of love I'm talking about now.
Physical love, that impulse that drives you to someone special, as
well as love of the other person's being, his or her essence, as it were.
Carnal love and, well, call it sentimental love, the day-to-day caring
about the other person. But sometimes I have a hard time accounting
for the fact that I must have loved my first wife too. But I did, I know
I did. So I suppose I am like Terri in that regard. Terri and Ed." He
thought about it and then he went on. "There was a time when I
thought I loved my first wife more than life itself. But now I hate her
guts. I do. How do you explain that? What happened to that love?
What happened to it, is what I'd like to know. I wish someone could
tell me. Then there's Ed. Okay, we're back to Ed. He loves Terri so
much he tries to kill her and he winds up killing himself." Mel
stopped talking and swallowed from his glass. "You guys have been
together eighteen months and you love each other. It shows all over
you. You glow with it. But you both loved other people before you
met each other. You've both been married before, just like us. And
you probably loved other people before that too, even. Terri and I

have been together five years, been married for four. And the terrible thing, the terrible thing is, but the good thing too, the saving grace, you might say, is that if something happened to one of us—excuse me for saying this—but if something happened to one of us tomorrow, I think the other one, the other person, would grieve for a while, you know, but then the surviving party would go out and love again, have someone else soon enough. All this, all of this love we're talking about, it would just be a memory. Maybe not even a memory. Am I wrong? Am I way off base? Because I want you to set me straight if you think I'm wrong. I want to know. I mean I don't know anything, and I'm the first one to admit it."

"Mel, for God's sake," Terri said. She reached out and took hold 58
of his wrist. "Are you getting drunk? Honey? Are you drunk?"

"Honey, I'm just talking," Mel said. "All right? I don't have to be 59
drunk to say what I think. I mean, we're all just talking, right?" Mel
said. He fixed his eyes on her.

"Sweetie, I'm not criticizing," Terri said.   60

She picked up her glass.   61

"I'm not on call today," Mel said. "Let me remind you of that. I 62
am not on call," he said.

"Mel, we love you," Laura said.   63

Mel looked at Laura, He looked at her as if he could not place her, 64
as if she was not the woman she was.

"Love you too, Laura," Mel said. "And you, Nick, love you too. 65
You know something?" Mel said. "You guys are our pals," Mel said.

He picked up his glass.   66

Mel said, "I was going to tell you about something. I mean, I was 67
going to prove a point. You see, this happened a few months ago, but
it's still going on right now, and it ought to make us feel ashamed
when we talk like we know what we're talking about when we talk
about love."

"Come on now," Terri said. "Don't talk like you're drunk if 68
you're not drunk."

"Just shut up for once in your life," Mel said very quietly. "Will 69
you do me a favor and do that for a minute? So as I was saying,
there's this old couple who had this car wreck out on the interstate.
A kid hit them and they were all torn to shit and nobody was giving
them much chance to pull through."

Terri looked at us and then back at Mel. She seemed anxious, or 70
maybe that's too strong a word.

Mel was handing the bottle around the table.   71

"I was on call that night," Mel said. "It was May or maybe it was 72
June. Terri and I had just sat down to dinner when the hospital called.
There'd been this thing out on the interstate. Drunk kid, teenager,
plowed his dad's pickup into this camper with this old couple in it.
They were up in their mid-seventies, that couple. The kid—eighteen,
nineteen, something—he was DOA. Taken the steering wheel
through his sternum. The old couple, they were alive, you understand. I mean, just barely. But they had everything. Multiple frac-
tures, internal injuries, hemorrhaging, contusions, lacerations, the
works, and they each of them had themselves concussions. They
were in a bad way, believe me. And, of course, their age was two
strikes against them. I'd say she was worse off than he was. Ruptured
spleen along with everything else. Both kneecaps broken. But they'd
been wearing their seatbelts and, God knows, that's what saved them
for the time being."

"Folks, this is an advertisement for the National Safety Council," 73
Terri said. "This is your spokesman, Dr. Melvin R. McGinnis, talking." Terri laughed. "Mel," she said, "sometimes you're just too
much. But I love you, hon," she said.

"Honey, I love you," Mel said. 74

He leaned across the table. Terri met him halfway. They kissed. 75

"Terri's right," Mel said as he settled himself again. "Get those 76
seatbelts on. But seriously, they were in some shape, those oldsters.
By the time I got down there, the kid was dead, as I said. He was off
in a corner, laid out on a gurney. I took one look at the old couple and
told the ER nurse to get me a neurologist and an orthopedic man and
a couple of surgeons down there right away."

He drank from his glass. "I'll try to keep this short," he said. "So 77
we took the two of them up to the OR and worked like fuck on them
most of the night. They had these incredible reserves, those two. You
see that once in a while. So we did everything that could be done,
and toward morning we're giving them a fifty-fifty chance, maybe
less than that for her. So here they are, still alive the next morning. So,
okay, we move them into the ICU, which is where they both kept
plugging away at it for two weeks, hitting it better and better on all
the scopes. So we transfer them out to their own room."

Mel stopped talking. "Here," he said, "let's drink this cheapo gin 78
the hell up. Then we're going to dinner, right? Terri and I know a new
place. That's where we'll go, to this new place we know about. But
we're not going until we finish up this cut-rate, lousy gin."

Terri said, "We haven't actually eaten there yet. But it looks good. 79
From the outside, you know."

"I like food," Mel said. "If I had it to do all over again, I'd be a 80
chef, you know? Right, Terri?" Mel said.

He laughed. He fingered the ice in his glass. 81

"Terri knows," he said. "Terri can tell you. But let me say this. If 82
I could come back again in a different life, a different time and all,
you know what? I'd like to come back as a knight. You were pretty
safe wearing all that armor. It was all right being a knight until gun-
powder and muskets and pistols came along."

"Mel would like to ride a horse and carry a lance," Terri said. 83

"Carry a woman's scarf with you everywhere," Laura said. 84

"Or just a woman," Mel said. 85

"Shame on you," Laura said. 86

Terri said, "Suppose you came back as a serf. The serfs didn't 87
have it so good in those days," Terri said.

"The serfs never had it good," Mel said. "But I guess even the 88
knights were vessels to someone. Isn't that the way it worked? But
then everyone is always a vessel to someone. Isn't that right, Terri? But
what I liked about knights, besides their ladies, was that they had that
suit of armor, you know, and they couldn't get hurt very easy. No cars
in those days, you know? No drunk teenagers to tear into your ass."

"Vassals," Terri said. 89

"What?" Mel said. 90

"Vassals," Terri said. "They were called vassals, not vessels." 91

"Vassals, vessels," Mel said, "what the fuck's the difference? You 92
knew what I meant anyway. All right," Mel said. "So I'm not educated. I learned my stuff. I'm a heart surgeon, sure, but I'm just a
mechanic. I go in and I fuck around and I fix things. Shit," Mel said.

"Modesty doesn't become you," Terri said. 93

"He's just a humble sawbones," I said. "But sometimes they suf- 94
focated in all that armor, Mel. They'd even have heart attacks if it got
too hot and they were too tired and worn out. I read somewhere that
they'd fall off their horses and not be able to get up because they
were too tired to stand with all that armor on them. They got tram-
pled by their own horses sometimes."

"That's terrible," Mel said. "That's a terrible thing, Nicky. I guess 95
they'd just lay there and wait until somebody came along and made
a shish kebab out of them."

"Some other vessel," Terri said. 96

"That's right," Mel said. "Some vassal would come along and 97
spear the bastard in the name of love. Or whatever the fuck it was
they fought over in those days."

"Same things we fight over these days," Terri said.   98

Laura said, "Nothing's changed."   99

The color was still high in Laura's cheeks. Her eyes were bright.   100
She brought her glass to her lips.

Mel poured himself another drink. He looked at the label closely   101
as if studying a long row of numbers. Then he slowly put the bottle
down on the table and slowly reached for the tonic water.

"What about the old couple?" Laura said. "You didn't finish that   102
story you started."

Laura was having a hard time lighting her cigarette. Her matches   103
kept going out.

The sunshine inside the room was different now, changing, get-   104
ting thinner. But the leaves outside the window were still shimmer-
ing, and I stared at the pattern they made on the panes and on the
Formica counter. They weren't the same patterns, of course.

"What about the old couple?" I said.   105

"Older but wiser," Terri said.   106

Mel stared at her.   107

Terri said, "Go on with your story, hon. I was only kidding. Then   108
what happened?"

"Terri, sometimes," Mel said.   109

"Please, Mel," Terri said. "Don't always be so serious, sweetie.   110
Can't you take a joke?"

"Where's the joke?" Mel said.   111

He held his glass and gazed steadily at his wife.   112

"What happened?" Laura said.   113

Mel fastened his eyes on Laura. He said, "Laura, if I didn't have   114
Terri and if I didn't love her so much, and if Nick wasn't my best
friend, I'd fall in love with you. I'd carry you off, honey," he said.

"Tell your story," Terri said. "Then we'll go to that new place,   115
okay?"

"Okay," Mel said. "Where was I?" he said. He stared at the table   116
and then he began again.

"I dropped in to see each of them every day, sometimes twice a   117
day if I was up doing other calls anyway. Casts and bandages, head
to foot, the both of them. You know, you've seen it in the movies.
That's just the way they looked, just like in the movies. Little eye-
holes and nose-holes and mouth-holes. And she had to have her legs
slung up on top of it. Well, the husband was very depressed for the
longest while. Even after he found out that his wife was going to pull
through, he was still very depressed. Not about the accident, though.

I mean, the accident was one thing, but it wasn't everything. I'd get up to his mouth-hole, you know, and he'd say no, it wasn't the accident exactly but it was because he couldn't see her through his eye-holes. He said that was what was making him feel so bad. Can you imagine? I'm telling you, the man's heart was breaking because he couldn't turn his goddamn head and *see* his goddamn wife."

Mel looked around the table and shook his head at what he was going to say. 118

"I mean, it was killing the old fart just because he couldn't *look* at the fucking woman." 119

We all looked at Mel. 120

"Do you see what I'm saying?" he said. 121

Maybe we were a little drunk by then. I know it was hard keeping things in focus. The light was draining out of the room, going back through the window where it had come from. Yet nobody made a move to get up from the table to turn on the overhead light. 122

"Listen," Mel said. "Let's finish this fucking gin. There's about enough left here for one shooter all around. Then let's go eat. Let's go to the new place." 123

"He's depressed," Terri said. "Mel, why don't you take a pill?" 124

Mel shook his head. "I've taken everything there is." 125

"We all need a pill now and then," I said. 126

"Some people are born needing them," Terri said. 127

She was using her finger to rub at something on the table. Then she stopped rubbing. 128

"I think I want to call my kids," Mel said. "Is that all right with everybody? I'll call my kids," he said. 129

Terri said, "What if Marjorie answers the phone? You guys, you've heard us on the subject of Marjorie? Honey, you know you don't want to talk to Marjorie. It'll make you feel even worse." 130

"I don't want to talk to Marjorie," Mel said. "But I want to talk to my kids." 131

"There isn't a day goes by that Mel doesn't say he wishes she'd get married again. Or else die," Terri said. "For one thing," Terri said, "she's bankrupting us. Mel says it's just to spite him that she won't get married again. She has a boyfriend who lives with her and the kids, so Mel is supporting the boyfriend too." 132

"She's allergic to bees," Mel said. "If I'm not praying she'll get married again, I'm praying she'll get herself stung to death by a swarm of fucking bees." 133

"Shame on you," Laura said. 134

"Bzzzzzzz," Mel said, turning his fingers into bees and buzzing 135
them at Terri's throat. Then he let his hands drop all the way to his
sides.

"She's vicious," Mel said. "Sometimes I think I'll go up there 136
dressed like a beekeeper. You know, that hat that's like a helmet with
the plate that comes down over your face, the big gloves, and the
padded coat? I'll knock on the door and let loose a hive of bees in the
house. But first I'd make sure the kids were out, of course."

He crossed one leg over the other. It seemed to take him a lot of 137
time to do it. Then he put both feet on the floor and leaned forward,
elbows on the table, his chin cupped in his hands.

"Maybe I won't call the kids, after all. Maybe it isn't such a hot 138
idea. Maybe we'll just go eat. How does that sound?"

"Sounds fine to me," I said. "Eat or not eat. Or keep drinking. I 139
could head right on out into the sunset."

"What does that mean, honey?" Laura said. 140

"It just means what I said," I said. "It means I could just keep 141
going. That's all it means."

"I could eat something myself," Laura said. "I don't think I've 142
ever been so hungry in my life. Is there something to nibble on?"

"I'll put out some cheese and crackers," Terri said. 143

But Terri just sat there. She did not get up to get anything. 144

Mel turned his glass over. He spilled it out on the table. 145

"Gin's gone," Mel said. 146

Terri said, "Now what?" 147

I could hear my heart beating. I could hear everyone's heart. I 148
could hear the human noise we sat there making, not one of us moving, not even when the room went dark.

THE STORY OF AN HOUR
Kate Chopin

Knowing that mrs. mallard was afflicted with a heart trouble, 1
great care was taken to break to her as gently as possible the news of
her husband's death.

It was her sister Josephine who told her, in broken sentences; 2
veiled hints that revealed in half concealing. Her husband's friend
Richards was there, too, near her. It was he who had been in the
newspaper office when intelligence of the railroad disaster was
received, with Brently Mallard's name leading the list of "killed." He
had only taken the time to assure himself of its truth by a second
telegram, and had hastened to forestall any less careful, less tender
friend in bearing the sad message.

She did not hear the story as many women have heard the same, 3
with a paralyzed inability to accept its significance. She wept at once,
with sudden, wild abandonment, in her sister's arms. When the
storm of grief had spent itself she went away to her room alone. She
would have no one follow.

There stood, facing the open window, a comfortable, roomy arm- 4
chair. Into this she sank, pressed down by a physical exhaustion that
haunted her body and seemed to reach into her soul.

She could see in the open square before her house the tops of 5
trees that were all aquiver with the new spring life. The delicious
breath of rain was in the air. In the street below a peddler was crying
his wares. The notes of a distant song which some one was singing
reached her faintly, and countless sparrows were twittering in the
eaves.

There were patches of blue sky showing here and there through 6
the clouds that had met and piled one above the other in the west facing her window.

She sat with her head thrown back upon the cushion of the chair, 7
quite motionless, except when a sob came up into her throat and
shook her, as a child who has cried itself to sleep continues to sob in
its dreams.

She was young, with a fair, calm face, whose lines bespoke 8
repression and even a certain strength. But now there was a dull stare
in her eyes, whose gaze was fixed away off yonder on one of those
patches of blue sky. It was not a glance of reflection, but rather indicated a suspension of intelligent thought.

There was something coming to her and she was waiting for it, ₉
fearfully. What was it? She did not know; it was too subtle and elusive to name. But she felt it, creeping out of the sky, reaching toward
her through the sounds, the scents, the color that filled the air.

Now her bosom rose and fell tumultuously. She was beginning ₁₀
to recognize this thing that was approaching to possess her, and she
was striving to beat it back with her will—as powerless as her two
white slender hands would have been.

When she abandoned herself a little whispered word escaped ₁₁
her slightly parted lips. She said it over and over under her breath:
"free, free, free!" The vacant stare and the look of terror that had followed it went from her eyes. They stayed keen and bright. Her pulses
beat fast, and the coursing blood warmed and relaxed every inch of
her body.

She did not stop to ask if it were or were not a monstrous joy that ₁₂
held her. A clear and exalted perception enabled her to dismiss the
suggestion as trivial.

She knew that she would weep again when she saw the kind, ₁₃
tender hands folded in death; the face that had never looked save
with love upon her, fixed and gray and dead. But she saw beyond
that bitter moment a long procession of years to come that would
belong to her absolutely. And she opened and spread her arms out to
them in welcome.

There would be no one to live for her during those coming years; ₁₄
she would live for herself. There would be no powerful will bending
hers in that blind persistence with which men and women believe
they have a right to impose a private will upon a fellow-creature. A
kind intention or a cruel intention made the act seem no less a crime
as she looked upon it in that brief moment of illumination.

And yet she had loved him—sometimes. Often she had not. ₁₅
What did it matter! What could love, the unsolved mystery, count for
in face of this possession of self-assertion which she suddenly recognized as the strongest impulse of her being!

"Free! Body and soul free!" she kept whispering. ₁₆

Josephine was kneeling before the closed door with her lips to ₁₇
the keyhole, imploring for admission. "Louise, open the door! I beg;
open the door—you will make yourself ill. What are you doing,
Louise? For heaven's sake open the door."

"Go away. I am not making myself ill." No; she was drinking in ₁₈
a very elixir of life though that open window.

Her fancy was running riot along those days ahead of her. Spring ₁₉
days, and summer days, and all sorts of days that would be her own.

She breathed a quick prayer that life might be long. It was only yesterday she had thought with a shudder that life might be long.

She arose at length and opened the door to her sister's importunities. There was a feverish triumph in her eyes, and she carried herself unwittingly like a goddess of Victory. She clasped her sister's waist, and together they descended the stairs. Richards stood waiting for them at the bottom. 20

Some one was opening the front door with a latchkey. It was Brently Mallard who entered, a little travel-stained, composedly carrying his grip-sack and umbrella. He had been far from the scene of accident, and did not even know that there had been one. He stood amazed at Josephine's piercing cry; at Richards' quick motion to screen himself from the view of his wife. 21

But Richards was too late. 22

When the doctors came they said she had died of heart disease— of joy that kills. 23

ODE TO MY SOCKS

Pablo Neruda

MARU MORI BROUGHT ME
a pair
of socks
which she knitted herself
with her sheepherder's hands,
two socks as soft
as rabbits.
I slipped my feet into them
as though into
two cases
knitted
with threads of
twilight
and goatskin.
Violent socks,
my feet were two fish made
of wool,
two long sharks
sea-blue, shot
through by one golden thread,
two immense blackbirds,
two cannons
my feet
were honored
in this way
by these
heavenly
socks.
They were
so handsome
for the first time
my feet seemed to me
unacceptable
like two decrepit
firemen, firemen
unworthy
of that woven

fire,
of those glowing
socks.
Nevertheless
I resisted
the sharp temptation
to save them somewhere
as schoolboys
keep
fireflies,
as learned men
collect
sacred texts,
I resisted
the mad impulse
to put them
into a golden
cage and each day give them
birdseed
and pieces of melon.
Like explorers
in the jungle who hand
over the very rare
green deer
to the spit
and eat it
with remorse,
I stretched out
my feet
and pulled on the magnificent
socks
and than my shoes.
The moral
of my Ode is this:
beauty is twice
beauty
and what is good is doubly
good
when it is a matter of two
socks
made of wool
in Winter.

CREDITS

1. The Environment

"The Obligation to Endure," from SILENT SPRING by Rachel Carson. Copyright © 1962 by Rachel L. Carson. Copyright © renewed 1990 by Roger Christie. Reprinted by permission of Houghton Mifflin Company. All rights reserved.

"The Next Step for U.S. Climate Change Policy," by Warwick McKibbin and Peter Wilcoxen. Reprinted by permission of the Brookings Institution.

"U.S. Forest Conservation May Increase Deforestation Elsewhere," by Pam Mayfield.

"Big Mac and the Tropical Forests." Copyright © 1985 by MR Press. Reprinted by permission of Monthly Review Foundation.

"Gas Guzzling Americans irk Europeans," by Derrick Z. Jackson in the *Boston Globe*, July 28, 2001. Copyright © by *Globe Newspaper* (MA). Reprinted with permission of *The Globe Newspaper*.

2. The Media

In Canada: From Brave New World Revisited by Aldous Huxley, published by Chatton & Windus. Reprinted by permission of the Random House Group Ltd. In the United States: "Propaganda Under a Dictatorship" (pp. 47–57) from BRAVE NEW WORLD REVISITED by ALDOUS HUXLEY. Copyright © 1958 by Aldous Huxley. Reprinted by permission of HarperCollins Publishers Inc.

"15 Questions About the Liberal Media." Copyright © 1995 by Jeff Cohen and Norman Solomon.

"Family Life," from THE PLUG-IN DRUG, REVISED AND UPDATED-25TH ANNIVERSARY EDITION by Marie Winn, copyright © 1977, 1985, 2002 by Marie Winn Miller. Used by permission of Viking Penguin, a division of Penguin Group (USA) Inc.

"The Coolhunt," by Malcolm Gladwell. Used by permission.

3. The Arts

"Why the Record Industry is in Trouble," by Jann S. Wenner. From *Rolling Stone*, September 19, 2002 Copyright © Rolling Stone LLC 2002. All Rights Reserved. Reprinted by Permission.

"Cop Out? The Media, 'Cop Killer,' and the Deracialization of Black Rage (Constructing [Mis]Representations)," by Christopher Sieving. From the *Journal of Communication Inquiry*, Volume 22, Issue #4.

"Born in Fire: A Hip-Hop Odyssey." From *The UNESCO Courier*, July/August 2000.

"Understanding Youth, Popular Culture, and the Hip-Hop Influence," by Patricia Thandi Hicks Harper as appeared in SIECUS Report, June/July 2000, Vol. 28, Issue #5, pp. 19–23.

4. Technology

From FLESH AND MACHINES by Rodney A. Brooks, copyright © 2002 by Rodney A. Brooks. Used by permission of Pantheon Books, a division of Random House, Inc.

From HIGH TECH HERETIC by Clifford Stolls, copyright © 1999 by Clifford Stoll. Used by Permission of Doubleday, a Division of Random House, Inc.

Danet, Brenda. 1998. "Text as Mask: Gender, Play, and Performance on the Internet." From *Cybersociety 2.0: Revisiting Computer-Mediated Communication and Community* edited by S. G. Jones. Thousand Oaks, CA and London: Sage.

5. Gender and Race

"The Girls of Gen X," by Barbara Dafoe from *The American Enterprise*. Reprinted with permission of *The American Enterprise*, a magazine of Politics, Business, and Culture.

"Wears Jump Suit, Sensible Shoes, Uses Husband's Last Name," by Deborah Tannen, *The New York Times Magazine*, June 20, 1993, copyright © Deborah Tannen. Reprinted by Permission. Originally titled, "Marked Women, Unmarked Men," by the author.

"Just Walk on By," by Brent Staples, from *Harper's*, December 1986. Reprinted from permission of the author.

6. Literature and Language